FOREWO

I am not a Hampshire man. I am a neighbour, born in Crowthorne just three miles over the County's northern border. But an inquisitive man knows a lot about his neighbours and I count myself sufficiently well travelled in Hampshire to impart an impartial and objective view on some of the hostelries therein.

I also count myself as one of the foremost of the nation's pub crawlers, having visited at least 13,000 licensed establishments in the country. Many of these were in Hampshire, and its close proximity to my home made the county a fertile watering ground for my numerous meanderings.

I have enjoyed a second home at Hayling Island for nearly 40 years and claim to be a regular in many of its pubs and clubs. The Island's neighbours; Langstone, Havant, Horndean and Rowlands Castle are also regularly encompassed by my infractious alcoholic crusades. In the north of the county, in such villages as Hartley Witney, Eversley, Yateley and Fleet my countenance is not unfamiliar to any landlord who has been around for more than a month or two.

All this to justify a Berkshire man's perusal and comment on the haunted pubs of Hampshire. I hope it will suffice. As to the witnessing of anything supernatural personall, I must answer in the negative. I did however, meet many sincere people who had witnessed things that could be judged a little strange.

Most stories in this book have been based on fact or the teller's interpretation of what is known of the facts. I am not here for adjudication or to offer any scientific evidence. These are colourful old stories of ancient hostelries and the first function of tale and teller to amuse. If, as with these stories there is an element of truth, so much to the good. I hope you enjoy reading them as much as I enjoyed researching them.

Roger Long

Local history from the same publisher

A Century of Cinema in Dorset
Famous Women in Dorset
Ancient Stones of Dorset

Also by Roger Long

Murder In Old Berkshire 1990
I'll be hanged 1991
The Crowthorne Chronicles 1992
Haunted Inns of the Thames Valley 1993
Final Commitment 1994
Ancient Berkshire Inns and their Stories 1996

1st edition published September 1999

ISBN 1 898073 16 3

Power Pulications
1 Clayford Ave
Ferndown
Dorset BH22 9PQ
Email: powerpublications.freeserve.co.uk

Publisher's Note

Whilst every care has been taken to ensure the accuracy of all the information contained in this book neither the author nor the publisher can accept responsibility for any mistakes that may occur.

Photographs: Brenda Allaway and Mike Power
Cartoons: Brenda Allaway
Compilation: Les Howard
Layout: Graham Whiteman
Printed by: The Baskerville Press, Salisbury, Wiltshire

CONTENTS

POPLAR FARM INN
ABBOTTS ANN, NORTH ANDOVER

*Abbotts Ann is an ancient and attractive hamlet on the outskirts of Andover.
It is speculatively one of the oldest Roman settlements in Great Britain.
It certainly possesses a Roman villa, The tessellated floor of which was removed tile by tile
and reassembled in the British Museum.*

Abbotts Ann's supernatural occurrences however, are not associated with the villa but with the Poplar Farm Inn. The building, which is some 450-500 years old, was originally a farm cottage, and so it remained for the vast majority of its long existence.

Rumours abound about previous tenants and equally various are the explanations of the supernatural activity which occurs there.

Villagers will tell you that it was once owned by a lady of society who kept it for orgies and revelries of debauchery. The drunken saturnalias lasting for days on end and shocking the local peasantry.

There would seem to have been no untimely end inflicted upon this hedonistic sybarite. In fact there is no record of her birth or demise whatsoever. If the parties did indeed take place, they must have been enjoyed by a dedicated few, for the rather contracted dimensions of Poplar Farm Inn would have prevented many from indulging.

There is also a story that the old building was used by smugglers and that the stories of haunting were invented to put off the inquisitive. This was definitely the case for some of our coastal hostelries but I deem it unlikely for one so far in land. In argument to this the locals will explain that the Poplar Farm Inn was a safe house used by smugglers in transporting goods from the coast to the capital. They will substantiate this by explaining the existence of an underground passage between the inn and the nearby River Anton (some say the River Pill). I am always sceptical about underground passages. I find it unlikely that the expense of their construction would justify their usefulness. It is not however impossible that the Poplar Farm Inn was used as a place of concealment, and conceivably also as a means of escape.

A local builder bought the old cottage in 1965 and turned it into a six bed roomed home for his family using materials from the nearby Littleton Manor at Fyfield.

In 1967 inexplicable sounds began to emulate from certain rooms. Doors would open and shut when no one was around and footsteps would be heard in corridors.

Christmas 1968 was a prime example, ghostly noises were experienced on an almost daily basis and these unexplained happenings lasted spasmodically for the next decade. The only visual experience being a sighting of a lady like shade in flowing attire (which resembled that of the late 18th century), 'gliding' up the stairway.

Since the mid 1970's supernatural noises have become less frequent but the occasional unaccountable noise still manifests itself on the unsuspecting.

Incidentally Abbotts Ann also possesses one of the country's spectral black dogs commonly known as shucks. There are some three dozen regularly reported, the Abbotts Ann one being particularly realistic. So much so that a local took a swipe at it with his cane which passed completely through the spectre.

THE CROWN HOTEL

ALTON, HAMPSHIRE

At the time of writing Alton has been mentioned as one of the five towns in England that is enjoying the greatest increase in house prices. The attraction no doubt is it's geographical location. This most pleasant of market towns is some 25 miles outside the urban sprawl of the Capital but within easy reach by train or road.

Alton revels in an extremely colourful history, a cottage in Amery Street, was the home to Edmund Spenser the poet. Spenser, who gave the country "The Faerie Queene" and the "Shepherds Calendar" resided here in 1590. He later died in poverty.

A far less honoured citizen of Alton was one Frederick Baker. I August 1869 Baker kidnapped and murdered a small child named Fanny Adams. A name that has been adopted into the English language; meaning of small value, insignificant or worth next to nothing. Fanny's body was discovered in the hills above Alton, it had literally been hacked to pieces. Limbs had been cut off as had ears and fingers. Eyes had been removed as had the intestine, not a pretty sight. The news spread to the Portsmouth Naval Dockyards where sailors were being introduced to a new diet of diced beef.

Some mariner with a morbid sense of humour likened the beef to poor Fanny's body and so the phrase "Sweet Fanny Adams" was born. Incidentally Baker was hanged at Winchester for his crime.

Now, less of Alton's grim past and more of the public house.

The signboard of the Crown is probably one of the most common in England. In bygone days many of the King's stewards and footmen retired with lumpsums.

Almost without exception they took public houses.

It was the done thing to honour ones benefactor, hence the popularity of "The Crown"

tomers dogs. They would bark aggressively whilst retreating, always staring at the chimney in the same place. The dogs displayed the typical canine attitude of hating something and fearing it at the same time. Barking at the unseen protagonist, when at a safe distance, but terrified of being pulled too near. Refusing to approach the chimney breast however persistent their master might be.

A previous landlord and several of his customers stated that they had regularly heard scratching from the other side of the wall. Speculation of course was rife. Older regulars related the tale of a drunken customer, who being tired of his dog continuously whining for him to leave the establishment, picked the poor creature up by it's back legs and dashed its head against the chimney breast.

The Crown Hotel at Alton was the venue for one of the country's very unusual canine hauntings. Whereas dogs are recognised to be extremely sensitive to the presence of the paranormal, for one to actually make itself known as one is rare if not unique.

A chimney breast at the Crown seemed to act as a catalyst in activating all sorts of frenzied behaviours in cus-

Throwing the lifeless body in the corner the man returned to his drink.

All good healthy speculation no doubt. What is not speculation and a fact that gives you resolute substance to the tale is that in 1967 workmen were involved in alterations at the establishment. They removed a false wall and the original dining room hearth was discovered. Close by lay the skeleton of a dog.

THE WHITE HART
BRIDGE STREET, ANDOVER

Andover as a settlement has been around since the Stone Age. Longbarrows have been discovered beside the Anton together with mysterious ditches that seem to have been a type of prehistoric irrigation system. the Romans were also here, and buried villages have been discovered beside the remnants of ancient roads. The Saxons were here and held a Witenage (National Assembly). In 994 A.D. Ethelred and Alphege entertained a Viking king here and convinced him to leave England in peace.
In it's more recent history, Andover became famous for it's many inns. It was on several staging routes and was a convenient place to stay for the night.

The White Hart at Andover is one of the many hostelries throughout the country that purports to have supplied board and lodging to Charles I. The epicurean father of the Merry Monarch however, must vie with Henry VIII, Good Queen Bess and Dick Turpin with having sampled the delights of every ancient inn.

Ancient nevertheless being a fitting adjective for the White Hart. It is at least 300 years old and in all probability somewhat older.

Incidentally, the "White Hart" sign board vies with "The Crown" for being the most popular in the country. It is taken from the badge of Richard II, a monarch much approved of by the populace, hence the numerous signs. On many "White Hart" sign boards the animal is adorned by a golden collar. The most unlikely story relates that an unnamed monarch was out hunting when he was given an exciting run for his money by a splendid white stag. The beast being finally surrounded and the king being so pleased with the sport that he freed the hart after placing a gold collar around it's neck and forbidding it to be hunted again. I have heard this story in a dozen or so White Harts around the country. What balderdash! Call me a cynic but the placing of a gold band around a stag's neck in a land full of half starving peasants would ensure it's demise within a few minutes.

Whether Charles I ever frequented its historic interior is debatable but a supernatural inhabitant has been witnessed on many occasions. It is an attractive lady in a dark green cloak or dress. She seems to favour bedroom number 20 where, in the 1960's she appeared to a female resident twice in the same evening. The double visitation was too much for the startled lady who checked out the following morning.

The green woman would seem not to be the only spectral intruder. There are also a couple of blurs thought to be an accompanying lady and gentleman, they seem to restrict their supernatural perambulations to the ground floor. A startled barman who once witnessed these two, described them as off-white and semi transparent and they disappeared before his eyes.

Whether it was the green lady or the semi transparent couple or a third phantom as yet unspecified that chased a petrified maid along a corridor is unknown. Footsteps followed the terrified serving girl up the stairway and along the corridor. She rushed into her bedroom and barricaded the door. The footsteps stopped outside. It was some time before the poor girl could be enticed outside again.

THE WHITE HART

LONDON ROAD, BASINGSTOKE

*F*or an explanation of The White Hart please refer to "White Hart, Andover"

Basingstoke is an old town made new by vast commercial and residential development. Many of it's attractive old pubs became fatal casualties of war. I suppose this is inevitable in what's generally called "progress". However, if one negotiates successfully the ring of numerous near impenetrable roundabouts one still may came across pockets of resistance.

The White Hart is a fine example. It stands erect and proud, albeit held hostage between it's large modern and characterless neighbours.

Rebuilding work in the late 1960's seems to have resurrected the supernatural inhabitants of the White Hart at Basingstoke. In 1968 a former landlady heard what could best be described as a barrel being rolled along a gravel path. This continued on a regular basis and always seemed to take the same route. On checking the stock there was found to be nothing missing. There was no possible way of entering the storeroom from outside and no gravel path in the near vicinity.

The phantom barrel rolling continued. It was experienced by two independent witnesses, both residents. One was so badly affected that he insisted on keeping his light on all night.

Spasmodically strange happenings continued. The gravelly noise occurred inside the inn. It approached the landlady's sister in her room. The noise seemed to go over the occupant and continue on its way. Not surprisingly the lady deemed it prudent to change rooms.

she was alone in the room. Most disconcerting.

Possibly down to coincidence was the demise of the unfortunate landlady's pets. Shortly after the partial rebuilding her cat got run over. One of her Great Dane dogs became ill and died. The other became vicious and had to be put down.

Perhaps whatever was in residence in the pub should have been left undis-

Many of the staff experienced what is known as a 'presence.' An odd job man heard footsteps behind him whilst he was bottling up. He turned with a start to find nobody there.

The strange audible evidence was to be followed by several apparitions. In the early 1970's the landlady's mother awoke to see a figure (gender unspecified) smoothing its hair. After completing the performance it disappeared. In 1975 a waitress was surprised to see a blonde girl's face reflected in the mirror when

turbed. There are countless examples of hauntings and poltergeist activity coinciding with structural changes to old buildings. Who knows.

And what of the old inn's history. Well, within living memory the hostelry was kept by two old sisters, one a spinster and the other a widow. One of the sisters (which one is not clear) died under very suspicious circumstances. No action was ever taken, nothing could be proved. I don't suppose it has any bearing on the hauntings but one never knows.

THE DOLPHIN INN

(ONCE CALLED THE GARRISON)
HIGH STREET, BOTLEY

The sign board of The Garrison is unusual, and, as it's name suggests is found without exception in towns that once possessed a military encampment. The village, (now thankfully bypassed) has narrowly escaped the urbanisation of Southampton. Much of Botley's centre has remained intact. Prestigious houses, quaint shops and attractive inns can still be found.

Botley's most celebrated citizen was William Cobbett, he of the famous "Rural Rides". But Cobbett had an enemy in Botley. One Richard Baker a self-righteous and overpowering parson. It was Baker who refused to release the church keys to the villagers thereby thwarting their intentions to ring the bells to celebrate Cobbett's release from Newgate. The villagers however got their own back by sending the parson post-haste to London. Baker had received a fraudulent letter from the Capital informing him of a non-existent legacy. Whilst their parson was absent the villagers enjoyed three days of unrestricted sport and indulgence.

Probably because of the many battles and skirmishes of the civil war Hampshire has a glut of spectral cavaliers. There must be some 20 or more reported within the confines of the county. One often wonders why no Roundheads, accepting of course the exception of Cromwell himself who is reputed to walk the ruins of Basing House.

The Garrison Inn at Botley was associated with a ghostly Cavalier for many years. Sightings however, were rare and even those that were witnessed seemed prone to exaggeration.

It seems unlikely that the weird shape that disturbed the landlady in 1980 had anything to do with the Civil War. It was described as 'a funny outline dashing past' later the adjectives 'tall' and 'slim' were added to the description. Various other paranormal phenomena followed. Footsteps were heard outside a bedroom door, there were also noises emanating from the cellar. It sounded so strong that it was first thought that somebody was ransacking the place.

The landlady's remedy to these supernatural disturbances was to hang a crucifix in the hall. The effectiveness of this is unknown but the spiritual experiences gradually abated. There is nevertheless, a cold spot in the dining room, with reports of a lower temperature in this particular place and the feeling of an indescribable presence.

P.S.
On a recent visit to the premises I had noticed that the name had reverted to the original "Dolphin".

TUDOR ROSE INN
BURGATE, NORTH FORDINGBRIDGE

The sign of the Tudor Rose is a very ancient one. It celebrates the end of the "War of the Roses" Henry of Richmond, head of the house of Lancaster, adopted the red rose as his symbol. After his victory at Bosworth in 1485, he became Henry VII. A year later he married Elizabeth of York thereby uniting the two houses. The marriage and the anticipated peace was greatly appreciated and celebrated. When Henry adopted a new emblem by superimposing a white rose upon a red one, "The Tudor Rose" was adopted as a trade sign by countless innkeepers.

Burgate is a tiny hamlet bestriding the A338 some three miles north of Fordingbridge. The Tudor Rose is a delight to behold, it is the epitome of an Olde English inn. It is half timbered and thatched and renown for it's pleasing countenance and warm hospitality.

The Tudor Rose is a 14th century coaching inn, once named La Chaumiere. It is steeped in history, however nothing untoward concerning the supernatural took place until the late 1960's. Once again it appears to be inexplicable noises and vague shapes. A team of experts from the Parapsychology Laboratory stayed at the inn. The investigators heard the noises but could not account for them.

Apparently the audible phenomena has diminished over the years but the shape occasionally puts in an irregular appearance. It has become accepted and now frightens no one.

QUEENS HEAD
BURLEY

The vast majority of the Queens Heads commemorate the crowning of Elizabeth I. However, any famous Queen up to and including Victoria may be immortalised on this board. There are also a specialised few that take a rather morbidly comical outlook. Commemorating as they do the Queens in history who have been unlucky enough to lose their heads. A couple of Henry VIII 's wives spring to mind.

Burley is one of the more remote and definitely more mysterious parts of The New Forest. Here is the eerie purple moor land, the treacherous bogs and blasted oaks (one strangely named "Naked Man" is a well-known landmark). This is the land of witchcraft and smugglers: the realm for warlocks and magicians. Here was the home of Brusher Mills the Snake Catcher and the wild enigmatic Gypsies with their piebald ponies.

The present Queens Head was built in 1660 and enjoyed a rather chequered existence. It's stoic and tacit clientele asking and expecting no questions. There were stories of ghostly noises exuding from beneath the building. The local highwaymen, who plied their trade from a nearby hill named Mark Way, proliferated and exaggerated the ghostly

tales. A frightened populace stayed in at night and did not get in the way of "Gentlemen's" nefarious affairs.

I have no idea if the floor of the Queens Head exudes it's ghostly whines but I do know that during rebuilding work an unknown cellar was discovered. Unknown! It was probably known to the "Gentlemen" centuries ago.

WHITE HART
CADNAM

For an explanation of "The White Hart" sign please refer to the entry at Andover.

Cadnam is a delightful village on the periphery of The New Forest where the M27 ceases and becomes the A31. It is also where these two roads are met by a massive roundabout by the A337 that takes holidaymakers to Lyndhust, Brockenhurst and Lymington. This is a junction to be avoided in summer at all costs. How out of place the impatient exhaust belching modernised traffic looks when one glances at the thatched and sedate Sir John Barleycorn just a stone‚s throw away.

The Sir John Barleycorn has a unique fame of its own. It has bedecked the front covers of a dozen books on the New Forest and has been the subject of a hundred different postcards. However, this time it is not the renowned Sir John Barleycorn we have come to visit. It is its lesser known neighbour a little further down the road.

At the White Hart in Cadnam there is yet another phantom lady, and once again the phenomena is experienced rather than witnessed.

The approach of this surmised glamorous lady is announced by the overpowring aroma of expensive perfume. The preceding haunted fragrance is followed by an almost sensual swish of silk. Then, as with most presence's it is accompanied by the almost inevitable drop in temperature.

A previous landlord who was an avid collector of clocks reported to Guy Playfair (a writer and investigator of the supernatural) that a long dormant antique clock started ticking when this lady approached.

There is no clue as to the lady's identity in the pub's history. A lady, probably beautiful and sensuous, arrogant and certainly cold, in all likelihood terrified that inescapable age would tarnish her beauty.

All this gleaned from a swish of silk and a whiff of perfume.

RED LION
CHALTON

The sign of "The Red Lion" is an extremely popular one and comes from the badge of the much exalted John O'Gaunt.

Chalton is a tiny hamlet a stone's throw away from the Sussex border. It's lofty position in the Butser Hills gives Chalton spectacular views. On a clear day Spithead, Hayling Island and The Isle of Wight are easily discernible. For its size Chalton has many pleasurable assets. It has Elizabeth Country Park with its attractive walks and has recently constructed a mock Iron Age village. A unique and tranquil windmill gazes down upon the traffic of the A3. Chalton also possesses an 800 year old church and it is because of this building that Chalton obtained it's inn, the oldest in the county.

When the church was being constructed in 1147, the stonemasons (a profession notorious for its thirst) insisted on a small building in which to sleep and quaff good ale.

Probably one of the country's most attractive pubs the Red Lion is the venue for what can only be described as a weekend haunting. The sound of knocking was heard near a chimney breast, exclusively on a Saturday. The landlord being a matter-of-fact type of chap, not given to the fanciful waftings of the supernatural, did the practical thing and engaged an archaeologist of his acquaintance.

The archaeologist came out with a theory, which can only be politely defined as far fetched. His imaginative explanation involved there being a vein through the chalk on which the Red Lion was built. This vein acted as an underground conductor and brought sound from a presumed but unidentified building some way away. In this envisaged building a man spent his Saturdays throwing logs into a wood-burning stove.

Joan Foreman investigating this case in the late 1970's discovered that the house opposite the Red Lion has been the victim of psycho kinetic (poltergeist) activity. However much one denies the existence of ghosts, psycho kinetic activity has been witnessed and recorded for some hundreds of years, and now even the most hard-headed realist must accept its existence even if its explanation is still in its infancy.

Reading reports on the case I have no doubt that the tapping at the Red Lion was in some way connected with the house opposite. Joan Foreman however, found it impossible to establish the accuracy of the reports from the house and once again things must be left to conjecture.

Incidentally, there are reports of a spectre horse and cart just down the road from the inn.

THE GREYFRIAR
CHAWTON

The sign of The Greyfriar is very unusual and in all probability named after a gentleman of the Franciscan Order of Monks. Try as I might I have been unable to trace the individual friar that gave his name to the inn at Chawton. I knew there to be an abbey at Alton and a priory at Odiham but Chawton would seem to have nothing monastic whatsoever. I should love to have unearthed the story of some mendicant brother begging his way around the country lane at Chawton unfortunately I have not.

Chawton basks in the praise of it's more famous abode "Jane Austen's House", the renowned authoress apparently resided here for the last seven years of her life. The trouble with places like this is as soon as the weather takes a turn for the better they are a Mecca for camera swinging, over appreciative elderly people with time on their hands.

It was such a crowd, an octet of the above described that I followed into the Greyfriar, the pub's unfortunate site being directly opposite Jane Austen's abode. I heard from locals long ago that there was some sort of supernatural activity here and I had intended to break my own rules and inquire of the landlord.

Whilst I waited impatiently for my fellow customers to order tea individually, sandwiches individually and then finally pay individually I had more than sufficient time to peruse the interior.

Obviously a landlord who has done much research into his establishment. Certain historical facts were imparted from table mats and notices upon the wall.

The Greyfriar was mostly 18th century although parts of it could be traced back to the 16th. It has also encompassed a bread or grocery shop next door. Somewhere along the lines of its long existence and many landlords the name had been changed to The Greyfriar. There was no word of explanation as to why.

I approached the young man who was by now less busy with the needs of the elderly. "I have been reading your history" I said "have you any idea why the name was changed to The Greyfriar, doesn't haunt the place does he?". "I have no idea why the premises changed it's name sir, as far as hauntings go several past landlords have reported some inexplicable experiences. Personally I've seen or heard nothing. If I had I would run a bloody mile."

That is my full knowledge of any supernatural activity at The Greyfriar at Chawton.

HOGS LODGE
CLANFIELD

Clanfield has several pubs of note. One down in the centre of the village, The Rising Sun, proudly boasts that it was built in a day. To all intents the boast is a sincere one. Terrapin type sections were delivered on the previous day. But were, in truth all assembled within the same 24 hours.

The Rising Sun however is not the hostelry that we are about to discuss.

Well out of the village on what used to be the old A3 London - Portsmouth road stands the isolated Hogs Lodge. High in the hills, near Butser, with magnificent views over the Queen Elizabeth Country Park, the Hogs Lodge sits resplendent in its remoteness.

The inn is now a landmark, a Mecca for robust hiking clubs. But once, before it was by-passed it was a highly respected and necessary oasis. A40s Anglias and Vauxhall Wyverns with a great deal of courage but less than perfect cooling systems would attain the top of the hill with a sense of achievement. In the 1950's charabancs (coaches) would apply first gear at the bottom of the hill and maintain it to the top, ignoring the screaming gear box.

The Hogs Lodge is not such an

ancient building as one would expect. The beamed and plaster exterior and the leaded lights are most deceptive. The inn is in fact some 75 years old.

There is something else deceptive here. It is the sign. Nowadays it shows the countenance of a gleeful and well over nourished porker. Naturally enough one may think considering the hostelry's name. Unfortunately not, for the word 'Hog' in this context refers to the old English word for burial place. And that's where the Hogs Lodge stands, right in the centre of an ancient Iron Age cemetery.

It was no accident the siting of the mock Iron Age village at Clanfield in the early 1990's. Above Chalton, Clanfield and Hambledon is a plethora of Iron Age forts and burial grounds. There is an ancient grave to an early British warrior high in the hills. Vague mystery surrounds this area and an atmosphere prevails that some people find overpowering.

Is it one wonders, this lone spearman's shade, that noiselessly strides across the Hogs Lodge's gravel car park on foggy nights. One can but wonder.

CROWN & CUSHION
COVE, MINLEY

The Crown & Cushion on the Cove/Minley road was once a tiny ale house. In the 1980's it was redeveloped into a complex containing a vast baronial hall.

Thomas Blood was born in Ireland in 1618. He came from a fine family, his grandfather being Edmund Blood of Kilnaboy Castle, County Clare.

Blood entered England during the Civil War. enlisting firstly with the Royalists and then with the Roundheads as Cromwell seemed to be succeeding.

Fighting bravely for the Parliamentarians he was given the rank of Colonel. After the war Cromwell bestowed a large estate upon Blood and made him a Justice of the Peace. He then married a Lancashire heiress who soon gave him a son. Blood seemed set for life.

Unfortunately for Blood, Charles II was restored to the throne in 1660. Taking a very dim view of the Royalists who had turned against him he confiscated Blood's lands and the good colonel found it prudent to return to Ireland with the utmost haste.

In Ireland Blood became a cattle rustler and highwayman. A thorn particularly in the flesh of Lord Armaband of Dublin. The Cromwellians were reforming in Ireland and Colonel Blood was once again involved.

During the war with the Dutch in 1665 Blood returned to England and through pure audacity achieved a position of high standing. It was strongly suspected that he was spying for Holland. Surviving the war, the plague and fire of 1666 we find Blood on the run once more.

He went to ground in 1666, not resurfacing until 1670 at Romford now calling himself Ayloffe and practising as a physician.

The medical cover was to disguise the Colonel's more nefarious activities as a gentleman of the road. On one of his nightly exploits he was felicitous enough to hold up the coach of Lord Ormond at St James Palace. On discovering who the occupant was he attempted to personally hang him at Tyburn. The good lord was saved by his servants and Blood found himself once more on the run.

In 1671 Blood put into practise his most audacious of plans. Disguised as a clergyman he had cultivated the friendship of one Talbort Edwards, the 77 year old keeper of the Crown Jewels at the Tower of London. The gems were kept in the Martin Tower and the Edwards family, father, mother and daughter, lived above.

It had taken months for the 'preacher' to get acquainted with Edwards but now the families were on the best of terms. Blood's recently acquired family comprised of a daughter, a young woman from Minley thought to be his mistress, and a couple of sons recruited from the criminal fraternity. One son, selected for his good looks, was about to be introduced to Edward's daughter with the intention of a betrothal.

After the robbery the plan was to ride post haste to the young woman's cottage at Minley, where they would hove up overnight before continuing through several safe houses to the Welsh coast and then on to Ireland.

On May 9th 1671 Parson Blood, accompanied by three young gentlemen, called upon the Edward's. Whilst one young man went upstairs to begin the courtship of Edwards daughter the other three men were shown the impressive Crown Jewels. Once down in the vault Parson Blood produced a mallet from under his cloak and set about belaying the keeper over the head and rendering him unconscious. The jewels were taken and the crown swiftly flattened with the mallet.

Unfortunately for Blood and his companions, Edward's son and several friends took that particular time to call upon the keeper and his wife.

Blood's 'son' ostensibly an ardent suitor, but in actuality a look out, gave warning from upstairs. By this time old Edwards had regained consciousness and was screaming for help. In a matter of minutes the Yeomen were on the scene and a prolonged and vicious engagement took place. Pistols blazed and no fewer than nine people were injured before Blood and his comrades were finally secured.

The above narrative is true and can be verified by any decent history book. The following is legend and conjecture.

Colonel Blood's mistress (acting

"THE COLONEL'S LATE. I HOPE HE'S BRINGING ME SOMETHING NICE."

daughter) waited patiently for his return from her tiny cottage in the woods beside the Minley/Cove road. By two in the morning she was in a distraught condition. By three she had received the news from another conspirator. Beside herself with the tidings of Blood's capture and imminent execution she drowned herself in a nearby lake.

Some time later the cottage became a pub. The Crown part of its name being obvious. Cushion being derived from the unfortunate lady's surname which had been Cushen or Cussens.

For some years the lady's shade was seen running about outside her cottage (pub) wringing her hands and deploring the fate of her lover.

Strangely enough the maiden's suicide was a little premature. Charles II found Blood such a likeable rogue that he pardoned him. There was also a rumour that the king had employed him to steal and then sell the gems abroad to cover his lavish style of living. Be that as it may Blood went on to enjoy an affluent and opulent lifestyle for a number of years.

THE HORNS
CRONDALL

The sign of the Horns is unusual and its origin is obscure. There are suggestions the sign came from the horns on a Viking helmet. I deem this most unlikely.

A somewhat more likely explanation is that before recognised signs, innkeepers hung objects upon their doors to advertise their establishments, i.e. The Crooked Billet would display a piece of carved wood or The Plough, an old plough share. Even this I find improbable, at least in the case of The Horns. I prefer the explanation that it is a shortened version of 'The Horn of Plenty', a well recognised inn sign in the 1800's. There is however one more tongue in cheek version, would you believe 'Horns of a Dilemma'. Shall I have another pint or go home to the 'missus'. Enough said.

Crondall was an ancient village much involved with the Civil War. There one of Hampshire's many ghostly Cavaliers is occasionally witnessed in the main street. Perhaps he is there to pay homage to a local philanthropist. Nicholas Love, a Parliamentarian, gave a substantial amount to rebuild the local church tower. Love was also a judge at the trial of Charles I but steadfastly refused to sign the death warrant.

The Horns is an inn that has much changed from the original. Internally it is now one bar and much of its quaintness has disappeared in the cause of efficiency. Its setting, situated some 100 ards off the Farnham-Odiham road, is leasant and secluded. The exterior can-ot be described as eye catching, but it as that homely country style and ambi-nce. The supernatural activity at The Horns is tenuous and largely born of hearsay. An ex-licensee once reported peculiar noises and unexplained foot-teps. There is no doubt a history here, but nothing has been tabulated and one grieves that possibly a dozen anecdotes have been lost in the mist of time, never to be resurrected.

The only really physical activity would seem to be in the early 1970's when a guest refused to sleep in the house after an unknown and presumed spiritual personage tugged at his hair.

This is not an unusual form of haunt-ing. If haunting indeed it is. I have been unable to interview this gentleman but it is possible that in many cases what is deemed to be an occult experience is merely a natural reaction. Arrectores picorum, is the condition when hair stands up on the head and the back of the neck. It is an involuntary reaction such as blushing. Not to take too sceptical a view on the phantom hair tuggers, but could it not be yet another chicken and egg situ-ation. One awakes in a fright, the hair stands on end extremely rapidly suggest-ing to the victim, in his semi-conscious state, that the hair tugging was the cause of his rude awakening and not the result of it. It's an idea anyway.

THE CHEQUERS INN
CROOKHAM

The sign of the Chequers is again a very popular one. The obvious explanation is the correct one. In the 17th and 18th century, landlords advertised that indoor games could be played at their establishments, much in the same way that darts and pool maybe advertised today.

This canal side public house is ancient indeed. There is some debate as to which came first, the pub or the canal. If my informants are correct this inn was run by the same family for some 180 years.

I first visited The Chequers some 30 years ago. It was our Holy Grail in those days to visit as many pubs as we could before the legal drinking age of 18. I personally achieved a staggering total of 1020 pubs before that legalised birthday. I remember descending on The Chequers on a bicycle after making half a dozen calls in Fleet and Dogmersfield.

My second visit to the old pub was whilst participating in a car rally cum treasure hunt in 1987. It was 7.30 in the evening, the sky was a sombre grey/black, thunder and lightening was everywhere. Under the circumstances the gaunt building looked the archetypal haunted inn.

Apparently the Chequers is haunted, albeit by a rather enigmatic presence. The only scant reference I can glean is that the shade is the spirit of a man who died on the premises as a result of a shotgun accident.

THE WHITE HART
DENMEAD

For an explanation of the "White Hart" sign please refer to the one given at Andover.

What can one say about this attractive inn nestling by the side of the busy B2150. It is old but not ancient, and was in all probability a coaching inn.

The interior is now more in keeping with the efficiency of serving meals and has that active potency that is associated with chains of eating houses. These groups provide a much needed service but no way would they sacrifice their shareholders profits by any indulgence towards the antiquated if inefficient structural design.

Managers of such inns are well groomed, attentive and polite, but they have neither the inclination nor the time to indulge in any but the shortest conversation with their customers.

Hence, when one has heard rumours that a certain hostelry has experienced some supernatural occurrences, what does one do? There is no A-Z of ghosts at the local library and the Yellow Pages has no listings. All one can do is return to the original source for evidence, and this may be enigmatic indeed. I quote from a lady:

"The White Hart at Denmead is haunted you know Rog' ."

"Is it indeed. By what or whom?"

"I don't know, but when we all used to drink there in the Seventies they all reckoned it was haunted. The landlord was sure of it."

"Oh, what kind of manifestations were there?"

"I don't know. A lot of unexplained noises and banging about."

That I'm afraid is all the evidence I have for anything supernatural occurring at the White Hart. Not a lot to go on is it?

A word of advice to the potential ghost hunter. Do not visit this establishment with any sense of confidence. If there was anything here in the 1970s, it has certainly been exorcised by the ultra efficient 1990s. It is however, a pleasant pub, you will enjoy your meal.

IZAAK WALTON
(ONCE THE NEW INN)
EAST MEON

*The Izaak Walton is named after the Country's most famous fisherman: The author of
'The Compleat Angler'. 400 feet above sea level the tiny River Meon rises.
It passes through the woodlands of the Forest of Bere before reaching Wickham.
It then meanders through chalk valleys adorned with farms and orchards for a further six
miles before finally reaching its destination at the Solent.
Walton knew every inch of it and spent much of his life here.*

East Meon is ancient country, the whole area is festooned with burial mounds and there is an Iron Age camp at the summit of Winchester Hill.

At Denmead the Bishops of Winchester held court. The medieval manor still exists that doubled as a courhouse. The red roof remains as do the charming ancient windows and time-worn timbers. Centuries of inclement weather has had little effect upon walls that are four feet thick.

At the Izaak Walton public house I am indebted to Joan Foreman for a story of a rather unusual nature. It concerns a thatched cottage that was once part of the New Inn's stables. Apparently there was a bolted door that had a habit of unbolting itself.

When a new family moved into the premises they discovered a door within a hollow wall. It led to an attic in which was found a small pair of soot encrusted boots. Obviously those of a sweep's chimney boy.

There has been for some time the feeling of a supernatural presence, but the evidence is thin and seems to comprise of a cat that would look up in a startled fashion, as if witnessing something that humans could not see.

Also when repairs were being made to a roof in the dining room it caved in, exposing a pile of lace bobbins that had been secreted between upper floor and ceiling. It has been suggested that the old building was once the home of a small cottage industry.

So there you have it. A door that unbolts itself, a startled cat, a batch of ancient lace bobbins and a pair of sooty boots. The ingredients of an eerie thriller, but what of the connection of these mysterious components. Very little I'm afraid.

THE GEORGE INN
EAST MEON

There are literally hundreds of pubs displaying the sign 'The George'. They may of course refer to any of the six gentlemen of that name who have ruled 'This Sceptred Isle! The law of probability suggests that the majority of these inns celebrate the reign of George IV, one of England's more popular monarchs.

This most delightful of Hampshire villages nestles between high chalk-capped hills. The slender River Meon, much frequented by Izaak Walton, meanders between ancient cottages.

Near a tiny humped back bridge stands the charming 17th century George, the archetypical village inn. Externally little has changed since the coaching days. The George's large chimneys and dormer loft windows with their colourful boxes seem conducive with Dickensian travellers. In ones mind's eye it is easy to imagine them thankfully dismounting, eager to vastly over indulge of the inn's plentiful fayre.

Internally the planners have made an exception of The George. An exception that unfortunately proves the rule with similar establishments. Various alterations over the years have complimented rather than contradicted the inn's antiquity. The three adjoining bars are cosy, comfortable and friendly.

There is also an indulgent open fire place where logs are reported to burn the whole year round.

An overall feeling of cosiness and well being cannot be denied, but what of the ghost that roams The George. A 17th century coachman I hear, who hanged himself in the kitchen.

I don't doubt that some poor soul hanged himself in the kitchen, but surely not a coach-man. That most kindly, con-vivial and courageous of breeds. Well fed and substan-tially bribed by the innkeepers to frequent their establish-ments. Men who could be in com-mand of any per-ilous situation on the road and turn any situation at the inn to their

advantage. Men who lived the prover-bial 'life of Riley', did not top them-selves. No, the poor spectre that not infrequently inflicted himself upon the George was certainly no coachman.

LE TOAD AND STUMPS
(ONCE THE LAMB)
EVERSELY

The name of Eversley is synonymous with that of it's one time curate, Charles Kingsley. Kingsley spent the vast majority of his life here and wrote 'The Water Babies' at the rectory. A true man of the people, his funeral was attended by Governors of Colonies, MP's, representatives of The Prince of Wales, bishops, deans, publishers, innkeepers, the Master of the Hunt, sailors, journalists, labourers and Gypsies from Eversley Common.

One wonders if the landlord of 'The Lamb' was present. It is known that Kingsley (a teetotaller) made frequent calls on the gentleman as part of his parish rounds.

This public house was called The Lamb for generations. Why it was necessary to change its name I have no idea. Being one of the nearer ones to my home village, just across the Berkshire border it has obviously been patronised by yours truly on a vast number of evenings sitting in front of the pub watching Eversley cricketers struggling against approaching nightfall.

It is a forever England pub and cricket pitch, unfortunately dissected by the busy A327 Reading to Farnborough road which was once a rutted track. As with all staging roads it was a dust bowl.

I should like to be able to tell you of a highwayman dying there after shooting it out with the authorities but I cannot.

However, the rumbling and gratings experienced in the 1950s and early 1960s at the inn were expounded by the local press as the meanderings of a regional highwayman. Most unlikely, this story scores one out of ten for factual evidence, but nine out of ten for romantic endeavour.

THE DAKOTA

FLEET

The council made the owners of this modern bar and restaurant move the gimmicky Dakota aeroplane tail from Fleet Pond. The waiters and waitresses will greet you at the door with a friendly Americanised 'Hi'. They will then announce their names and point out that your pleasure is their command. All very friendly, very clean and ultra efficient. The last place in the county you would expect to be haunted. And you'd be right, it's not.

But the bank on which it is built was supposedly so. Fleet Lake was the biggest fish pond in Hampshire. About three quarters of a mile long and covering 130 acres, the monks of St Swithins at Winchester used to fish here many years before the railway cut it in two.

The spirit, an attractive lady dressed in white, is enigmatic indeed. She lay dormant for over a hundred years before reappearing in the 1960's. The shade, probably a nun, may have had some clandestine assignation with one of the St Swithins monks, but we shall never know. All is supposition.

I made a return trip to the Dakota early one Sunday afternoon in February 1998. Kids were running everywhere with balloons and it was party time at two dozen tables. I moved to the bar for safety and ordered a pint of bitter. The barman seemed quite bemused by my request and pointed out that they did not do pints. Apparently, one could have a half a pint or a quart and 99% of his beer sales were lager. Am I really that archaic? Are we really approaching a time when a pint of beer will become as obsolete as a 'Goblet of Mead'. I sincerely hope not.

SURE ITS A RELIGIOUS SYMBOL BROTHER FRANCIS. IT APPEARED OVERNIGHT.

THE ALMA
HALE

The signboard of 'The Alma' commemorates the battle of that name in the Crimean War, other inn names of the same ilk are Balaclava, The Inkerman and The Sebastopol.

It is outside the Alma Inn, in Alma Lane, Hale, that the sound of heavy-booted running is heard. News of war, victory or defeat was once flashed from one beacon hill to the next. This form of communication preceded the telegraph towers. In fact it was about the time of Waterloo in 1815 that a sophisticated system of telegraph towers had been set up between the fleet in Portsmouth and the Admiralty in London. The thirteen hilltop semaphore stations could transmit the news over the 70 mile distance in a matter of minutes.

This however did not help the poor orderly who was despatched from Beacon Hill at Eweshot near Fleet. He was carrying the good tidings of Wellington's victory when he was waylaid enroute to Aldershot at a place now called Alma

Lane. There he was beaten to death by three footpads who relieved him of his money. So the story goes anyway.

We are not informed as to whether or not anybody was subsequently convicted of the murder. Or why the unfortunate man was picked upon. Soldiers were notoriously hard up in the early 19th century. Perhaps it was an opportune attack by three locals well into their cups and unable to indulge further through lack of funds. All again is speculation. It is also speculation as to whether or not the ghostly running footsteps that pass by The Alma late on a June evening actually belong to that unfortunate soldier.

HAYLING ISLAND

Hayling Island was once justifiably famous for its smugglers, pirates, inns, holiday camps, caravans and golden beaches. At the time of writing the smugglers have all but disappeared. The pirates are now cunningly disguised as estate agents and chalet landlords. The inns remain, some 20 at the last count. The holiday camps have become more refined and expensive (no hi-de-hi on H.I.). The caravans have proliferated to a menacing degree. The sandy beaches are still there, unfortunately they are under a forty foot thick, three mile long barrier of shingle. This being a two edged brainwave of the Authorities. It works well. It keeps both the sea and the holiday makers at bay.

THE NEWTOWN HOUSE HOTEL

This sedate old building lies near the middle of the island. In summer, it watches with whimsical dignity the endless parade of frustrated motorists that crawl by its walled extremities.

Some of the building is reputed to be Tudor but to my uneducated eye, the majority of the structure would appear to be Victorian. Unfort-unately there are some profit necessitated extensions of the 1980's but it has to be said to the Hotel's credit that they have been discretely hidden from general view. As with many an hotel, The N e w t o w n House started life as a private residence, a farm with stables. Beams in the older part of the house reputedly came from French ships that were sunk off our coast.

John Potter, a popular Irish barman and local character, once worked at The Newtown, and well remembers a little old lady calling at the establishment. This lady, a visitor to the island, claimed to have once lived there, in the days when it was a private house. Local homespun historians believe this to be just about possible. Little doubt was left on the sub-ject when the lady began to expound on the subject and described in some detail one of the bedrooms, her bedroom.

It was once again John Potter who told me of another lady visitor, the spectral blue lady. The blue lady has been witnessed fairly regularly in living memory. She passes (floats) noiselessly from room to room on the ground floor at the north side of the hotel, her special partiality being the corridor to the conference room that was once several bedrooms. "She wears a scarf and gown" said John.

"Surely you mean a cowl or veil" I replied, bearing in mind that 90% of female spectres are nuns wearing their obligatory habits.

"No Rog," he stated, "it's a dress and headscarf."

So, what do we make of that? Perhaps the Newtown ghost is a little more modern than most.

SMUGGLERS HAUNT
HAYLING ISLAND

This old established hotel has been owned and frequented by a number of famous people over the years, amongst which it is rumoured that it was patronised by Douglas Bader

I first came across it at the age of five while on one of those greatly looked forward to and often disappointing trips to the coast. In those days it was merely a restaurant called The Porch.

Breaking the rule for just this one occasion I approached the proprietress, a jovial and bubbly personality named Doreen Carver, a lady well known throughout the island.

I had heard the main outline of the story and unfortunately Doreen could add little more. Being Hayling Island the tale concerns smugglers. Over the years the place has been inundated with them and one could fill a volume with their exploits.

The yarn at the Smugglers Haunt concerns a young lady, name unknown, who was thought to be in league with the revenue men. Injustice was swift and permanent among the freebooters and the lass was quickly murdered. The way she was executed by the smugglers is un-clear but strangulation seems to be the favourite. Inevitably, as with all good stories, she was found to be innocent after her sad demise and is now said to haunt the building.

Unfortunately I cannot verify this story at all. With no names or dates where would one begin. It is a good yarn anyway.

There is also said to be a crypt full of brandy under the floor of the Smugglers Haunt. When this is mentioned in conversation with guests Doreen is often asked 'Why don't you dig it up?' Think of the expense, the inconvenience, the mess and loss of trade. Massive and costly excavation which may or may not reveal a secret crypt and a case or two of cheap French brandy. Not a viable proposition, and it might upset the spectre of the unfortunate lass. Let her rest in peace, she was wronged enough on this side of the curtain.

Now a private house, please respect the privacy.

CAT AND FIDDLE

HINTON ADMIRAL

The sign of the Cat and Fiddle is a corruption. The cat is said to be adapted from Caton, an English Knight who held Calais against the overwhelming French. Le Fiddle (the defender) is the second part of the sign. Obviously, over the years, Caton-Le-Fiddle could only be corrupted to the Cat and Fiddle.

Hinton Admiral is a tiny hamlet on one of the main New Forest roads in the vicinity of Christchurch.

The Cat and Fiddle is a thatched and partly cob built inn. It is believed to be one of the oldest hostelries in the country, being used by the Monks of Christchurch Priory as a place of refreshment for pilgrims.

The Cat and Fiddle was once the meeting place of Roden the Rider and his gang of smugglers. Many were finally caught and hanged nearby. It is thought that Roden and his gang were responsible for some nocturnal hauntings the Cat and Fiddle has experienced over the years.

Recently, The Cat and Fiddle has been brought by a steak house group and much of its individuality has gone. Its phantom smugglers have also disappeared. Draw your own conclusions.

THE OLD MILL

HOLBURY

The Hamlet of Holbury is so tiny it is only named on the area's more detailed maps. For those choosing to visit (a very worthwhile endeavour), head for the massive Fawley oil refinery and then ask a local.

A stranger such as myself discovers this hostelry with a sense of achievement. On the day I arrived, hailstones as big as golf balls were coming down in stair-rods. The Old Mill was hospitable, atmospheric and even cosy in spite of its spacious size.

I knew it would be pointless approaching the somewhat youthful staff with a view to discovering what supernatural occurrences had arisen. Such staff are busy and transient, strangely at odds with their historical surroundings.

Once again I must rely on legend and hearsay. The Old Mill was obviously not designed as an inn but, as the name suggests, a mill. However, the only reference I could find was that the building was a large 15th century cottage that has relatively recently been joined by a newer building.

There have been reports here of a ghostly monk, not unusual amongst supernatural beings. Monks and nuns vie with headless horsemen for being the most prolific inhabitants of the spectral world. This reported apparition is a little unusual in so much that he sports a bushy red beard.

THE WHITE HART

HOOK

For the explanation of the White Hart board, please refer to Andover entry.

Hook has a phantom Cavalier which seems to be a mandatory requirement of many Hampshire villages. This hamlet's Royalist shade appears to restrict himself to Hook Common where he has been witnessed dashing hither and thither in some sort of frenzy. One explanation is that he absconded from the affray at Old Basing and is in a turmoil whether to return to his comrades and risk death or capitulate to the far greater motivation of self preservation.

As far as we know it is not this conscience stricken shade that haunts the composed atmosphere of The White Hart.

The White Hart (not to be confused with the Old White Hart which appears to be a much younger establishment), is an ancient coaching inn on the A30. For some reason this hostelry has adopted a plethora of varying names over the centuries. Definitely it was once The Spread Eagle and also The Wyvern. There is also belief that it was known as The Crown and possibly The Bell. The main bar of The White Hart exudes an ambience of bygone abundance and content. It has

retained its original tiled floors and brick walls. Spits turn in the fireplaces at either end.

The ghost's domain is upstairs. 'Nellie', as she is affectionately referred to, is pleasant and friendly but has a tendency to be untidy. She has a habit of unlocking doors and leaving them open.

This unknown spectral lady has probably stayed insitu for a number of years, as several large extensions to the building, have given her a greater scope for her inquisitive activities.

THE SPIRIT IS UNWILLING
AND THE FLESH IS WEAK

RED LION

HORNDEAN

For an explanation of the 'Red Lion' board please refer to the Chalton entry.

If I have thoroughly overdone one phrase in this book it's 'attractive old coaching inn' but there is no other fitting description of the Red Lion at Horndean. It stands on a bend on the old A3, where the B2149 branches off for Havant and Hayling Island. The junction was a notorious bottleneck until the Horndean bypass was opened. It now enjoys a more sedate and unhurried existence. Much of its old world charm has returned.

The Red Lion was haunted by a little old lady in black. Her costume is that of the early 20th century and up until fairly recently the old girl put in regular appearances, often it seems at 8 in the evening.

The spectre was first witnessed by the landlady who mistook her for a customer in search of the loo. As she followed the old lady to give her directions the landlady was surprised to find she had disappeared.

The licensee's next altercation with the spectre was a little more ominous.

She sensed a presence willing her to jump from an upstairs window. Fortunately she was able to withstand the temptation.

There followed all sorts of supernatural phenomena. Doors opened and closed, customers felt shoves in the back, a barman heard the latch on the back door rising and lowering. The old lady was witnessed regularly on the steps that led to the cellar and also on her way to where a wash house had once stood. Her most frequent appearance being on the staircase that ascended to the first floor bedrooms.

After some research it was decided that the shade was that of an old lady named Mrs Byden who had died at the pub in the early years of this century.

Unfortunately the staircase prevented the coffin from being taken down and through the front door in the orthodox manner. It had to be unceremoniously pushed through a first floor window.

It is possible that old Mrs Byden took exception to this ungracious departure because, years later when the stairs were removed during internal reconstruction, the hauntings ceased. Nothing supernatural has been experienced for many years. There is however one small exception, a cold spot remains where the stairwell once stood.

Post Script:

While awaiting publication of this book, I came across a lady who was doing care work for my mother at Hayling Island. This lady informed me that she and her mother worked at The Red Lion at various times from the late 1980's until the mid 1990's. Both saw a spectre on several occasions. The manifestations varied between the cellar and the children's outside playground. The figure, described as vivid but also benign, was of a far younger lady than the one mentioned above.

Who said hauntings have to be logical? Are these two separate ladies or one lady in different stages of maturity? Interpretation is once again down to the reader.

THE CROWN
KINGSCLERE

For an explanation of 'The Crown' signboard please refer to the Alton entry.

I did a write-up on The Crown at Kingsclere in my book Final Commitment' so I shall not dwell upon it here. The story of the three murders at the premises was hushed up for nearly 30 years. Even now the facts are sparse and very difficult to obtain.

A brief outline of the story is as follows. American GIs stationed at Sydmonton Court in 1944 were rubbing locals up the wrong way. There had been burglaries, shop lifting and even rapes. Things had become so bad that a special report had been prepared for General Eisenhower in person.

Ten GIs from the above mentioned Sydmonton Court walked down the three miles to Kingsclere early one October evening. They entered The Crown where they were asked to show their passes by three or four American MPs. Failing to produce the said items they were ordered back to camp. On their arrival they straightaway armed themselves with rifles and returned to The Crown.

Secreting themselves behind the church wall opposite, the ten men opened fire on the public house. MPs Anderson and Coates died in the onslaught, as did the landlady Mrs Amelia Napper. A third MP Washington was also injured but he returned fire wounding two of the GIs.

That is just about the story, other than to relate that things were so well hushed up that even the local newspapers hardly dared touch upon it. It is however, known that nine out of the ten accused were convicted at a court martial in Thatcham and sentenced to life imprisonment.

I will admit that, although the story has been relatively well known to me for a number of years, I had no idea that The Crown was haunted until reading Guy Playfair's 'Haunted Pub Guide'. Unfortunately Mr Playfair, generally so meticulous in all his endeavours, omits to inform us by whom or what the establishment is haunted.

Having made my own enquiries in the area and having been unceremoniously escorted off Sydmonton Court by security guards, my cameraman Mr Peter Bourne and myself repaired to the pub.

All we could glean from recent management and ancient regulars was that the spirit is thought to be that of Private Anderson who lived long enough to leap through the window and return fire before expiring on the lawn.

A terrible and very involved story this one, but to the best of my knowledge and enquiries the spiritual evidence is almost negligible.

THE ROYAL OAK
LANGSTONE

*T*he majority of the countless boards that display this design were the result of a
national exuberance over the restoration of Charles II to the throne.
The oak was, of course, symbolic to his escape after the battle of Worcester. In the early
days the oak tree was considered sacred and was an inn sign in its own right. The Royal
being added after the Worcester escapade.

Langstone probably gives the visitor one of the finest aspects anywhere in the South of England. The mill with its old black tower, surrounded by any number of ancient buildings has been the cover feature of more books on Hampshire and the South of England than any other setting. It is pleasing on the eye, Langstone Harbour, there can be no doubt about it. From the Ship Inn on the Hayling Island bridge to the faraway slender outline of the remains of Warblington Tower, every building has a unique beauty and composure of its own.

Midway along this row of comely waterside fabrications stands the strikingly white Royal Oak.

The inn, in keeping with its environment, has suffered a good deal from media over-exposure during its long history. Its ghost, witnessed on very few occasions, has suffered the same fate. In fact at any time there must be a dozen spiritual anthologies indulging themselves with the supernatural happenings at The Royal Oak.

The offending spirit at the pub is yet another lady in white. After spending 20 spiritually uneventful years at the pub, in 1969 the landlady was awoken by a strange noise. She immediately suspected her daughter of sleepwalking, nocturnal somnambulism being a frequent habit of the young lady. The landlady inspected her daughter's room and found her safe in bed, however as she turned she was silently approached by the spectre of a tall woman dressed in white. The shade moved towards the stricken woman and then proceeded to glide completely through her before disappearing on the landing.

As far as it is known this is the one optical experience of the white lady at The Royal Oak. There is however, a possibility that there was a further sighting.

In 1970 a visitor who had booked a bedroom for a week left after one night. The man, obviously terrified, would only state that his room was haunted and that he had no intention of spending another night at the inn. He would be drawn no further and departed at haste.

Whether or not this man actually saw anything supernatural or had been spooked by the many inexplicable noises that have been regularly heard, we shall never know.

I give little credence to the story of an underground passage between The Royal Oak and Langstone Mill. A white lady is said to haunt the mill and slip along a secret passage to The Royal Oak between appearances. A sort of spectral

moonlighting. It has been my experience after examining a couple of dozen supposedly secret passages that the reason they keep non-existent their secret so well is that they are nonexistent. In this particular case anyone who knows Langstone Village must realise that the gap between The Royal Oak and the mill spends a goodly percentage of its time underwater. To attempt a subterranean passage under such shifting sand would be insane and totally futile. To put it another way - like trying to dig a hole in water.

There is another story at The Royal Oak that relates to a secret room being discovered at the turn of the century. I deem this to be unlikely. The Royal Oak is not a large building and the discrepan-cy between the size of the rooms and the external walls would have been notice-able from the day it was constructed.

There are however, further unex-plained sightings in the vicinity of The Royal Oak. An evangelist appears fairly regularly about 20 yards from the inn. He lays upon a grassy path, totally naked. Once witnessed, the spectre disappears in a flash, if you'll forgive my earthy sense of humour.

Who is this unique unclad and unrest-ed spirit? The evangelist (name unknown) was a homespun preacher with a missing leg. He limped around the vicinity of Langstone Harbour, supported by a crutch and carrying a heavy haver-sack. He would sit upon the nearest con-venient bank, seat or stone wall and call small groups to their religious reckonings.

This tall, painfully thin and gaunt man with a nose like Wellington and a countenance like thunder would inform his awe-struck flock as to what would happen to them in the next life, should they not hear his words and repent.

After his performance, the evangelist would distribute (sell) miniature Bibles and scripture cards from his haversack.

Perhaps not all of his flock took heed of the itinerant Good Shepherd for the story is that the evangelist was found murdered and robbed at the edge of the mud flats in Langstone Harbour. This would no doubt account for the spiritual preacher and possibly also his lack of attire.

Strange noises are still sometimes heard at The Royal Oak but as with many ancient buildings there could be a hundred boring but plausible reasons. Nevertheless I have a brief personal rejoinder concerning the old inn.

In my teenage years a gang of us used to use the pub quite regularly. We owned a house at Hayling Island at the time, and it was the done thing to catch a bus to Langstone in the early evening, quaff a pint at the Royal Oak, then sup another at every pub from there to the Hayling sea front.

This being a distance of some five miles, with nine or ten hostelries en route, one can imagine the state of yours truly and friends when the feat was finally accomplished. But I digress. One evening I was in the Royal Oak when I detected the aroma of fresh bread baking. I mentioned this to my comrades and all agreed they could smell the same thing. Not an unusual event you might think in this day and age when the bill of fare in most pubs is extensive.

In the early 1960's however this was not the case, the culinary manifestations of most establishments being confined to plain crisps or cheese rolls on the menu. This being the case we were surprised at such an appetising aroma, so much so we complimented the landlord upon it.

We were subsequently informed that there was no new bread upon the premises, least of all piping hot. So ended the conversation.

I believe I noticed the smell of new bread on two further occasions but mentioned it to nobody. It was then some years later that I acquired the knowledge that for the first part of The Royal Oak's 450 year history it was a bakery.

Could the spectral woman in white have been a baker's wife, or is that just a little bit too fanciful?

THE SWORDFISH

LEE ON SOLENT

Very ancient country is this, but by the clean and recent buildings of Lee on Solent one would be forgiven for doubting it. However, on the cliffhead numerous Iron Age tools have been discovered.

The Swordfish itself is no age at all. It is its position that is unusual and what makes it worthy of mention. The inn stands on Monks Hill, which, as its name suggests, was on the site of an ancient priory. It was from here that the brothers wended their way to the beach. And from the beach legend dictates that they took an ancient walkway to the Isle of Wight.

I have watched the tides here. I am by no means an expert on maritime matters, but unless things have greatly altered over the centuries, I find it difficult to imagine anyone 'walking' to the Isle of Wight without drowning. Still back to The Swordfish. The path that runs beside the inn has experienced melodic chantings on warm summer evenings. The sounds have been variously described as a moaning monosyllabic warble at one extreme to peaceful beguiling rapture on the other.

The more cynical, nay practical amongst us have ascribed the audible encounters to the wind eddying its way amongst the bushes on the hill. This is quite possibly true. Not having personally experienced the phenomena I shall withhold judgement.

Incidentally, The Swordfish takes its name from the famous torpedo bomber that played a starring role in the sinking of the German battleship Bismarck. It was also involved in an attack on the Italian fleet at Taranto.

HIGH CORNER INN

LINWOOD

The name of the High Corner Inn is obviously because of its geographical location.

t is some years since I have visited the High Corner Inn at Linwood. Although it is reasonably close to the busy A31, it is till a little difficult to find. The end result however justifies the means. It is a most attractive building overlooking the purple heather and pine trees of the New Forest. t gives one a feeling of stately remoteness rather than one of isolated desolation. Caught on a stormy or blustery night it is he archetypal venue for the spirit world.

In the 1970's two sisters from Southampton were working at the hostelry, and for convenience sake, staying at one of the chalets in the grounds. One of the young ladies awoke at 3 am o witness the shade of a middle-aged ady in period costume. Too terrified to wake her sister in case any harm should ome to them, the young girl lay inert, mesmerised by the figure.

The figure seemed to be standing, arms folded, staring through a glass panel in the door towards the stables. After about ten minutes it slowly disappeared.

Nobody could have entered the room as the door was locked. I've no doubt that the young girl witnessed something supernatural and was naturally terrified. What I am inclined to doubt is the time element. Ten minutes is a very long time for a manifestation to prolong its existence.

The average time for an apparition to reveal itself is between five seconds and one minute. Ten minutes would probably be a world record. No doubt in such situations time would seem to stand still and an error would be plausible and acceptable. It would no way invalidate the sincerity of the observation.

THE ROYAL ANCHOR HOTEL
LIPHOOK

*T*he sign of The Royal Anchor is probably unique and refers to the many royal personages who made this hostelry their overnight stopover or anchorage between London and Portsmouth.

For information concerning the haunting of The Royal Anchor Hotel I am again indebted to Guy Lyon Playfair. Mr Playfair being in turn indebted to Jack Hallam.

There is little information about this spirit, in fact it was only witnessed once, and then by one of our colonial cousins, a lady from Australia who happened to be staying in bedroom number 6, the haunted bedroom.

It is in this bedroom that local highwayman Captain Jacques was shot down by excise men while trying to escape Apparently the fugitive was desperately searching for a hidden door next to the fireplace. He failed to discover this concealed route of evasion and perished. I am not surprised that nobody has ever discovered it since.

If The Royal Anchor isn't haunted then it damned well should be. It has a pedigree as long a mayor's address, inundated with colourful figures of the past No less than eight British monarchs have visited the inn along with Queens f Portugal and Spain. The Prince Regent, Wellington and Blucher dined ere after Waterloo. Nelson frequented he place. Hardy visited it once on his ay to Portsmouth, prior to the victory t Trafalgar.

As with all old inns there is nevitably the suggestion of hidden underground passages, a phrase that lways sets personal alarm bells ringing. Whereas it always adds a little romance o a yarn, not one in 50 actually existed. hey are usually coupled with smuggling ales and as such totally impractical and nadequate. In Liphook's case why hould smugglers struggle some 15 to 20 niles across open ground with their ill otten gains, then to construct an under- round passage for the last couple of undred yards, it doesn't make economi- ally viable sense.

The Royal Anchor had vast cellars as nost inns did to keep the beer cool. It is also generally accepted that French pris- oners were chained there over-night, en route from Portsmouth to London.

But to return to the ghost. As men- tioned above, it is supposed to be the spec- tre of Captain Jacques, a local highway- man, complete with mask, cloak and French cocked hat. Once again romanti- cism at its worst. The Hollywood stereo- type of the highwayman does far more for his image than it does for establishing facts. There were no velvet coats, no Black Bess's, no jewelled pistols, no lace collar and cuffs and definitely no French cocked hats, not even Claude Dual possessed one.

There were assaults in the dark, cud- gels that pulverised brains and sharp knives that slit throats for a few pennies. If Captain Jacques did exist, reputedly on the Bosham and Langstone marshes, then he had very little to do with your Errol Flynn image and absolutely noth- ing to do with The Royal Anchor.

THE ANGEL
LYMINGTON

The sign of 'The Angel' is an ancient symbol connected to religion.
*It is derived from the salutation originally representing the Angel that appeared to the Holy
Virgin at the Annunciation.*

Lymington is a cheerful little town on the Boldre Estuary. Georgian houses are prevalent on the attractive and ancient streets. Yachts are still in abundance off the slipways but the days when Lymington's dockyards provided more ships than neighbouring Portsmouth have long since gone.

The 16th century coaching inn, The Angel (once The George), boasts two or possibly three unquiet spirits. Firstly is the sailor or possibly shipbuilder that appeared to a relief manager in the 1970's. He was described as tall and grey,

adorned in an old fashioned mariner's coat which displayed large brass buttons. This spectre appeared only the once, to one particular witness at 11.30 at night. The site where the inn now stands was once a shipbuilding site, as indeed was most of Lymington. Therefore it is local legend that the grey, bearded gentleman in question was involved in that occupation. However, I find one-off sightings a little suspect, there are too many of them. Hypothetically speaking is it likely that a family would dwell in an establishment for generations without witnessing the slightest spiritually untoward incident, then a man visiting for a few days should discover the local manifestation.

You may of course answer that it is well attested that some people are more susceptible to the supernatural manifestations than others. I cannot disagree with this argument but I still deem the bearded boat builder at The Angel a little unlikely.

The second shade at the inn has been witnessed on a number of occasions. It is the ghost of a coachman, who in the small hours of the morning pushes his nose against the kitchen window. Is this possibly some poor coachman eager to be away whilst thwarted by his passengers' indulgence at the inn. Or more likely, awaiting his free gratis victuals to be thrust through the window. We shall never know.

The third spectre takes the part of an unseen pianist. In 1966 the landlord's sister-in-law heard the ivory tinkling emulating from a downstairs drawing room.

Much to his annoyance the lady insisted that the landlord arose and searched the premises. This he did but the initiator of the haunting refrain was never discovered. There was, in fact, no piano in the building. Coincidentally there had been such an instrument on the premises right up until the lady's visit. It has been thrown out the previous day as it was in such disrepair. Strange.

Incidentally, in my maternal grandparents' house, named St Faith's at Sandhurst in Berkshire, it was not unusual for the old piano to play a couple of bars on its own. My mother was the fourth of five children that regularly heard it. They would creep downstairs in a posse, suddenly flinging the door open. The instrument would stop at that very second as if the pianist had been discovered. This was such a usual event that the children became insulated against it. Nocturnal detective forays became old hat and lost their appeal.

HURRY UP WITH MY VICTUALS, THATS THE SPIRIT.

THE GEORGE
ODIHAM

For an explanation of 'The George' signboard, please refer to the East Meon entry.

There are a dozen old stories woven into the fabric of Odiham, each leaving behind a reminder, a nostalgic token from the past. There is a Tudor vicarage. There are some almost disintegrated ruins, all that is left of an old palace once frequented by Elizabeth I. There is the famous old chalk pit that was quarried by the French prisoners of war. On the Winchfield road is the ancient Frenchman's Oak that denoted the extent to which the captive French officers were permitted to stray. And finally at neighbouring North Warnborough

stands the hollowed and mysterious Odiham Castle. Built as a hunting lodge for bad King John. It was from here in 1215 that he rode to Runnymede to sign the Magna Carta.

The imposing George inn is surrounded by many other noble buildings in this tiny, stately town. The Georgian facade belies its antiquity. A licence was granted in 1540, the year Henry VIII married Anne of Cleeves and Catherine Howard.

In the old inn's Oak Room, wattle and daub walls are exposed to view as if needlessly authenticating its venerate age. In another room, the restaurant, an impressive fire surround is supposed to have been taken from Basing House after Cromwell's relentless siege of 1645.

Over the centuries The George has doubled as an assize court complete with a convenient whipping post in an upstairs bedroom. Also as a cell for French prisoners of war. But it was neither of these rather colourful aspects that initiated the haunted associations of the inn.

It is a weird little story to say the least. Once upon a time, in late 19th century, The George employed a coachman to take its late night revellers to various parts of the district. The terrain was morose, uninhabited and desolate. Footpads frequented the coaching routes where life could be forfeited for the few shillings in a man's possession. It was little wonder that the coachman's young wife worried about him and often kept a silent, nervous vigil until his return.

One particular night the young woman believed she heard her husband's approach. Throwing back the door she was greeted by a lady in a long grey cloak. The face was hideous, no flesh remained, just the skull protruded from

the hood. The young wife watched in horror as the abominable spectre walked through the fence and was gone through the old inn's yard.

The young coachman did return about an hour later, quite unharmed. The wife however was in such a state of nervous hysteria that it was morning before she could be quieted.

The wife looked upon the hideous apparition as an omen. A warning of approaching death. She pleaded with her husband to give up his job. Eventually he agreed, anything for a quiet life, and took on a nearby ale house where they all lived happily ever after.

Incidentally, you will notice in the picture of The George a bike adorned with French onions. Photographer Peter Bourne and I visited The George on the day that the unappreciated red plonk Beaujolais is rushed across the Channel at breakneck speed. What cannot be seen in the picture but was nevertheless appreciated were two extremely leggy young ladies, sporting themselves in can-can attire. What's that old adage about men with no teeth looking at apples.

JOHN BARLEYCORN
PORTSMOUTH

*The John Barleycorn was the scene of a particularly nasty murder in 1943.
The landlady, Mrs Robinson, at 63 years old, did not trust banks. She took the takings to
bed with her each night in two old black leather handbags. This prudent habit of the
elderly lady was to bring about her demise. She was strangled one night in late November.
Her handbags containing some £450 went missing.*

The police were at a loss as to finding the perpetrator of the crime but the metropolitan police arrested an old lag for a trivial crime in the Waterloo Road about a month later. With no prompting whatsoever from the police, Harold Loughans admitted to the murder amongst various other crimes. He seemed pleased to get it off his chest. Talkative and chatty to the extreme Loughans seemed to have been plagued by conscience.

Things were to change however, when he finally appeared at Winchester assizes in March 1944. Loughans pleaded not guilty and assured the court that he had made the confession after being intimated by the police. The old lag had a badly deformed hand and the defence stated that it would be impossible for him to use sufficient force to strangle the unfortunate victim. The case was unique for it brought a head to head confrontation between the country's two foremost pathologists.

Sir Bernard Spilsbury in a very unusual role for the defence stated that he had tested Loughans strength in that hand and was of the opinion that he could not have committed the act.

Dr Keith Simpson for the prosecution

"STOW YOUR GAB WOMAN
I'M CATCHING THE MORNING TIDE"

ssured the jury that in his opinion oughan, had more than sufficient trength to perform such an action.

Spilsbury had reigned supreme for ecades. His opinions were never doubt- d and Harold Loughans was acquitted. On leaving court he was promptly arrest- d for a similarly vicious crime in Edgware. After years in prison for consec- tive crimes, Loughans approached The People newspaper in 1963. He offered hem his life story in which he admitted he murder at the John Barleycorn. Three months later he died aged 70.

There have been various bumps and ven the occasional screams detected from Mrs Robinson's bedroom over the ears. The knocks however dwindled and the screams became fewer in the 1950's and nothing has been reported since the early 1960's.

Once the Blue Posts at Portsmouth also boasted the ghost of an old fash- ioned seaman who had the disturbing habit of joining guests in their beds.

Another reputedly haunted inn was the Spotted Dog where John Felton murdered the Duke of Buckingham in 1628. There is an obelisk near Clarence Pier where Felton hung in chains. It was thought to be his ghost that haunted the old inn for decades. Unfortunately the Spotted Dog has joined the Blue Posts and the John Barleycorn, eradi- cated by progress, lost in the mists of time.

THE WHITE SWAN
PORTSMOUTH

The sign of the White Swan is again a very ancient and popular one. It can be traced back to 1349 when Edward III used the symbol on his shield and tunic before entering the annual tournaments at Canterbury. However, some schools of thought maintain that the swan was an inn sign long before this, it's noble bearing a symbol of innocence, and, therefore popular with landlords.

Lying virtually in the shadow of the city's guildhall, this extremely attractive pub boasts a rather nasty little story. A story that I was unable to authenticate. Deciding to have a word with the landlord (an unusual and generally unrewarding source) I made the mistake of visiting the White Swan on June 4th 1994. The 50th anniversary celebrations of D-Day were in full flow and the bar was throbbing with American sailors. Not a good time to arrest the landlord's undivided attention. This being the case I shall furnish the reader with the few facts that seem to be of general knowledge.

Sometime in the unspecific 1880's the White Swan employed a comely serving wench whose husband was a sailor. Speculation suggests that whilst her husband was away at sea this comely lady succumbed to several propositions from local gentlemen.

On the return of her spouse, a row ensued followed by a violent altercation that found the barmaid laying dead upon the hearth.

We are not informed by what means the sailor perpetrated this atrocity, but the general consensus of opinion, some 110 years later, is that he slit her throat with his splicing knife.

As the scene was witnessed by several customers I believe we can take it as read that the sailor was arrested and got his come uppance, but again there is no documented evidence of this.

The wraith of the serving wench, dressed in virginal white, was regularly witnessed, floating past the fireplace, the scene of the heinous crime. Although the lady had been a little reticent to show herself recently there is quite a well attested report of a sighting witnessed by the landlord's nephew in 1991.

CONNAUGHT ARMS
FRATTON, PORTSMOUTH

The name of the Connaught Arms is in recognition of the Duke of Connaught, a greatly admired local benefactor to the City.

Fratton was once the closest village to Old Portsmouth Town and therefore the first to be swallowed up by the metropolis. It is now famous for Fratton Park, the home of Pompey's football team.

As recently as 1987 the landlord of the Connaught's purchased a second-hand piano for his children. The first time the landlord noticed that there was something amiss was when his pair of fearless Rottweilers gave the instrument a wide berth. It was as if there was something constantly emanating from the piano. A sound that was above the human hearing range but detectable to the canine ear

On later occasions the family heard distinctive sounds coming from the piano and even when quiet it had an eerie awesomeness about it. To cut a long story short, the family straightaway sold the offending instrument and the Connaught Arms rested in peace.

There is a little more to say. This is obviously a tale of a haunted piano and not strictly one of a haunted pub. However, had I been the landlord I should have kept tabs on the new owner and made tentative enquiries as to whether he had witnessed any disquieting experiences.

LOOK ON THE BRIGHT SIDE LUV. IT SAVES US PAYING FOR A KARAOKE NEXT FRIDAY.

THE WHITE HORSE
PRIORS DEAN

Locally known as the pub with no name and also the initiative for a beer of the same instigation. If this doesn't make sense let me try and elucidate.

The White Horse is an attractive 17th century inn situated about 100 yards off a back road running from the A32 to Petersfield. Its remoteness adds to and exploits its charm. Edward Thomas, the pastoral poet, appreciated the inn's qualities and visited it on many occasions.

The White Horse has no sign, so one could pass within a hair's breadth without being aware of its existence, and hereby hangs the story of the "pub with no name." In all honesty it is legend rather than any spiritual occurrences

that qualifies the White Horse for it rather tenuous inclusion in this volume.

Many years ago (not specified), ar old gypsy woman was making her way to Alton from Petersfield. It was a terrible night, the wind was howling and the rair was like stair-rods. The poor womar could go no further when she noticed a light in the woods. Making her way to it she discovered The White Horse Asking the landlord for sustenance she was ordered from the premises. The old crone then beseeched the landlord to remain the night in the stables. This again was curtly refused. She took once more to the road but not before she had cursed the inn and denied the landlord the right to advertise his wares. Should he not remove his sign evil would befall him, was the gist of the curse from the lips of the old hag as she left the premises to sleep (some say to die) in the sodden woods.

Well that's the story. Whether anybody associated with ensuing landlords has ever come to grief I do not know. The sign at the moment of writing remains closeted, probably stashed in some garage somewhere.

The gypsy curse, absolute balderdash. It's a bit like the West Indian voodoo. If you believe in it, it psychologically causes you a certain amount of self inflicted harm. At the risk of repeating myself I have lived, fought, drunk and worked with gypsies since I was five years old. Attending dozens of weddings and funerals, and sitting up for nights with the bereaved. I have pulled Christmas trees, tottred, tarmac-adamed drives and sorted scrap iron in their company for donkeys years. On average I suppose I was cursed about three or four times a day. Nothing too untoward has happened to me yet - touch wood.

Actually the White Horse sign adorned the edge of the road for most of the 1950's, '60's and '70's. It could be spotted from a distance. In all probability the landlord removed it to discourage the multitude of coaches that used the road as a short cut to Hayling Island and Southsea.

WHITE HART & THE FOUR SEASONS

RINGWOOD

For an explanation of the White Hart board please refer to the Andover entry. Incidentally, the Four Seasons was a separate premises that has at times been absorbed by the inn.

Ringwood itself is a pleasant town on the banks of the salmon rich, River Avon. It was once the home of the usurper The Duke of Monmouth. Monmouth House is an unimpressive building in the High Street. After loosing the Battle of Sedgemoor, The Duke literally crawled on hands and knees to beg the pardon of James II. All to no avail, soon another head was to fall at Tower Hill.

These two adjoining buildings are possibly visited by the same spirit, a woman with flowing robes. The manifestations at the White Hart are sparse and obscure indeed. The Four Seasons restaurant,

which is no longer in existence, had a slightly more detailed apparition.

In 1973 a chef preparing food in the kitchen saw a lady in a long grey flowing robe walk past his open door. He called out but there was no reply. Being intrigued enough to make an inspection he found that there was nobody in the vicinity. Escape, without retracing back past the kitchen door, would have been virtually impossible.

At about this time there was a certain amount of mild poltergeist activity. Knives and forks rattling, cups and saucers breaking. The sort of things that could have had a perfectly reasonable explanation.

The chef was not the only person to witness the old lady in grey. Later a visiting folk singer saw her sitting on a chair at the top of the stairs. His shocked reaction was such that he fell from top to bottom. At the same instant a young girl reported an ice cold shiver in the spine'.

The old lady in grey is purported to be the proprietor of a sweet shop that was once part of the premises. She met an untimely demise under the wheels of a horse and cart. According to Anthony Brode in 'Haunted Hampshire' a medium was called in from Bournemouth but failed to make contact.

THE SWAN
ROMSEY

For an explanation of the sign board please refer to the White Swan at Portsmouth.

The Swan may no longer exist as an inn but the massive wrought iron sign still remains resplendent. The ironwork is long and very strong. The strength of the sign was tested in the 1640's. Lord Fairfax, a general in the Parliamentarian forces during the Civil War, stayed at Romsey. Fairfax, renowned as a disciplinarian, lodged at the Swan Inn. He found the wrought iron work conducive with hanging his deserters. The length and sturdiness allowing him to execute two at a time.

What could be more natural than tormented spirits of these men to haunt this makeshift gallows! Revellers over the centuries who have crossed the square at night have been instantly sobered by the brief and eerie sight of a struggling man.

It is difficult in a case like this to establish where fact and fiction meet. A venue such as this with an undoubted colourful history is often apt to bring out the more inventive parts of a vivid imagination.

Romsey is of course synonymous with Broadlands, the majestic house of Lord Mountbatten. A previous owner was Lord Palmerston whose bronzed statute, the work of Mathew Noble, stands bareheaded in the Town Square.

An ancient building near to the statue is now the Conservative Club. Once this attractive structure was an inn, the Old Swan Inn.

THE FOUNTAIN INN
ROWLANDS CASTLE

Rowlands Castle is the epitome of the English Village. It has a large green surrounded by terraced houses, and punctuated by newsagents, an ironmongers, a tiny post office, an even smaller bank and the inevitable couple of pubs!

One of these hostelries is the Fountain Inn. The origin of the Fountain as a pub sign goes back to the days of the Roman occupation and possibly even earlier. It denotes that there was a natural brook or spring near to the ale house and thereby inferred that the house brewed beer was purer and sweeter.

Personally, I used to visit Rowlands Castle a great deal. If the residents are to be believed the village is inundated with ghosts. Perhaps the villagers show respect because the phantom inhabitants seem to have them outnumbered.

The rectory is apparently haunted but whether this is the new one or old one, no one is quite sure. There is a path leading across a common towards Havant that is haunted by Charlie Peace. Yes - poor old Charlie again. According to village legend, Charlie was either sitting upon his horse drunk or dashing away from the authorities when he was struck across the throat by a low branch and died from his wounds.

I have spent most of my adult life

studying the history of 17th, 18th and 19th century villains. I have been lucky/talented enough to have three books published on the subject. Although there are ample substantiated historical entries on such renown highwaymen as Dick Turpin, Claude Duval and Colonel Blood etc., I have yet to unearth anything about Charlie Peace. There was a Charlie Peace, a rather nasty double murderer. But he was in the early part of the 20th century and as far as I can ascertain, he never rode a horse. The lack of existence has not stopped Hampshire people adopting Highwayman Charlie as their own. In the north of the county around Eversley and Yateley, he is virtually idolised.

Along the above mentioned path a shapeless mass appears and disappears from time to time putting the wind up any dog that happens to be present. Also late one evening the youthful attendant of an all-night filling station noticed something obscure travelling across the main Havant Road from the direction of the common. It scared the young man so much he handed in his notice.

However, I deviate, there are various other strange apparitions in Rowlands Castle but this is a book on haunted pubs and up to now I have refused to be side tracked. Perhaps the reader will forgive the above single misdemeanour.

Back to The Fountain. I have known the proprietor of this establishment for some years and have slept at the premises on several occasions. He was unaware that I was a writer and broadcaster (he could be right) and also unaware I was interested in the supernatural. This particular spirit cropped up in conversation one day. It is a female child some 12-14 years old who travels the long corridor that passes all the guest's bedrooms. The phantom seems neither cheerful nor depressed. She has a look of the Victorian era and is attired in a long garment, probably a nightie.

The landlord has never witnessed this young lady but heard about her when he took over the inn from the previous landlord. I am told that she has been the subject of several articles in the village magazine over the years. Unfortunately, thus far, I have been unable to trace one.

This Victorian child was last sighted in the corridor some dozen years ago. Never mind - next time I stay in bedroom number three I'll leave my door open.

THE FILLY INN
SETLEY

This is probably the only inn of this name in the country. It is certainly the only one that I have come across. My ancient dictionary's definition of a filly is a female foal or lively young girl. Which of the two this particular board commemorates, I was unable to ascertain.

The inn itself is splendid, and one of a rapidly dying breed. A wayside inn that was once regularly found between towns. They have been succeeded by Little Chef's and Happy Eaters. Unfortunately, but probably inevitably for survival, the atmospheric 'Filly' seems to see dining as more of a priority than wining.

It was not always so, the ancient purple moors of the New Forest surrounding the inn were both mysterious and perilous to the traveller. On this wild moor are the graves of the men that built the great earthworks at Buckland Rings.

Viewed from the top of Petersons lofty tower at nearby Sway, one may see a land little changed by the marches of time. Pleasant enough on a sunny day, but an enigmatic threat and even terror when a blood angry sun subsides. An obscure and unreasonable fear encompasses one in this richly atmospheric area.

The story of the hauntings of The Filly is brief but colourful. In the 19th century an unnamed wealthy traveller was journeying from Brockenhurst to Lymington to meet a ship. He was robbed and murdered by three sailors near a place named Cobblers Corner. His body, according to some reports, was casually thrown into the River Boldre. The newly affluent sailors repaired to the Filly Inn to liquidise their loot. The boasting of their deeds was overheard by the landlord who sent his potboy for the authorities. The sailors were surrounded, arrested, tried and sentenced to be hanged in chains. The rapidly decomposing bodies were left on gallows near the Filly Inn as a warning to others.

For many years their spirits were thought to roam the inn searching to reap revenge on the landlord. There seem to have been some sightings of these errant seamen in earlier days however.

THE WHITE LION

SOBERTON

The sign of The White Lion is yet another relic from the War of the Roses 1455 - 1471. The White Lion was the badge of Edward IV, very much of the Yorkshire camp. Landlords, being a particularly fickle crowd, a daub of paint could turn the White Lion into the Red Lion overnight, thereby appeasing which particular side had the upper hand at that specific period in time.

On the west side of the magnificent village church, amongst other gargoyles are the sculptured heads of a man and woman divided by a skull. Near to one head is a key beside the other is a pail. These two objects give credence to the village legend that the two heads represent a local butler and a dairy maid. This twosome's diligence and prudence managed to save nearly everything they earned and on their retirement built the tower of the aforesaid mentioned village church.

The one drawback to a total commitment over the years was the butler's partiality to a pint of good ale. If his wife (partner whatever) missed him in the evening she had only to repair to the local pub. There were however parts of the inn in which the butler could hide. And the lady in grey that periodically haunts the inn (nicknamed Lucy) is the shade of the dairymaid seeking the butler.

The story above is as I heard it. I do not vouch for the authenticity. I do not think the reader should investigate too deeply. For instance, one possible flaw is that the church tower may turn out to be older than the present White Lion. This would not necessarily invalidate the story, there may have been an earlier ale house here.

DOLPHIN HOTEL
SOUTHAMPTON

It would be futile of me to attempt to write a quick precis on a city as large and historically colourful as Southampton. There are a plethora of books on the subject in every library.

The sign of the Dolphin has several explanations. The most obvious being the inn's close proximity to the sea. Another explanation with nautical connotations is that the Dolphin represents one of the many trade associations, it was the crest of the Ancient Watermen. Finally, also with a nautical explaination, the ancients believed that the friendly dolphins were a type of primitive gale warning. They had the habit of making a floundering vessel more secure by wrapping themselves around it's anchor.

I have studied pubs for nearly four decades and one thing remains a total mystery to me. Why is it that landlocked counties such as Berkshire, Buckinghamshire, Oxfordshire and Hertfordshire etc., are inundated with such nautical signs as The Dolphin, The Ship, The Jolly Sailor and The Anchor?

The imposing Georgian facade of this central hotel belies its ancient roots. Part of the construction is Norman and there is said to be evidence of Elizabethan alterations. Its massive and impressive bow windows are reckoned to be the largest in the country.

The Dolphin was said to be on one of the earliest mail routes. A coach ran daily between the inn and the Swan With Two Necks in London.

The romantic ambience of the Dolphin has attracted the crowned heads of England and Europe over the years. The massive stables at the inn housed Queen Victoria's horses on her frequent visits to the Isle of Wight. Thackeray, Edward Gibbons and Jane Austen number amongst the Dolphin's illustrious clientele.

With all of these romantic figures from the past, it seems a bit of an anti-climax that the reputedly haunting spirit is a cleaning woman called Molly.

In the 1970's Molly glided two feet above the ground and was accompanied by a deep drop in temperature. Unfortunately Molly has not been witnessed recently. Perhaps she has finally moved upstairs.

THE RED LION
SOUTHAMPTON

What a wonderful old pub this is; almost unique in withstanding the tasteless modernisation of the centre of Old Southampton. It is situated in the High Street not far from the Dolphin. There is a themed pub stuck between them to remind what could happen when the large groups monopolise the whole of the trade: Unthinkable but more than likely.

The Red Lion's cellar is 12th century but the vast majority of the building is well preserved Tudor.

The Courtroom bar diplays a plethora of original exposed beams in and around the gallery. It also has a magnificent Tudor fireplace. A further attraction are the bar's walls, they are adorned by the Coats of Arms of the nobles who officiated at the famous trial of 1415. A list and explanation of the Arms is posted on a notice on the exterior of the inn.

Prior to his departure for Agincourt, the undercover agents of Henry V exposed three conspirators from within his ranks. Lord Scrope of Masham, Richard Earl of Cambridge and Sir Thomas Gray were tried and convicted at the courtroom of the Red Lion and were executed at Bargate, some 200 yards away.

With the death of such notable personalities one would have imagined some truly colourful hauntings. Unfortunately not. Over the centuries eye witnesses have reported a phantom mournful procession from The Red Lion to Bargate.

HARE AND HOUNDS

SWAY

*T*he sparsely populated and widely spread village of Sway is dominated by Thomas Peterson's 218 foot tower.

Peterson had quite a story. He was born in 1813, in Yorkshire, ran away to sea, became a lawyer, made a fortune, became a spiritualist and retired to Hampshire. Here he built his famous tower. Apparently, it was originally intended to be a mausoleum but Peterson's wife objected strongly. It was in India, where he had spent much of his life that Peterson had witnessed bodies being incarcerated above ground in towers and his 'folly' at Sway was for his own glorification.

There were, of course, other reasons for this thirteen storied construction. One was that it gave much work to local men. This did not endear Peterson to the local gentry, who complained that he overpaid his men. Another reason was that this extremely slim and tall structure was built almost entirely of con-

crete, a product that was in it's infancy in 1878/9 and needed to be proven. The original construction had a light at its head but Peterson was forced to remove this as it was mistaken for a lighthouse and a danger to shipping.

Now to one of Sway's inns. The Hare and Hounds stands a little outside the village, close to a cattle gridded entrance to the New Forest. There is very remote haunting here. Nearby was once the Marlpit Oak where a gallows stood. Three outlaws were hanged there and it is their grim procession to their demise that is thought to be responsible for the phantom procession that has been witnessed crossing the inn's car park.

I hasten to add that the sightings were always rare. I do not believe there have been any in living memory.

BRUSHMAKERS ARMS
UPHAM

The Brushmakers Arms is over 600 years old. In its somewhat chequered history is has been a one man broom factory, a school, a private house and finally a public house. Apart from being commandeered in 1664 by Oliver Cromwell for his regional headquarters.

The original owner was an old miser named Chicket. He made besoms by day and derived pleasure from counting his considerable profits by night. His horde was kept under his bed and this led to his downfall. Legend has it that a thief broke in and took the old man's savings and his life. The sound of the miser walking and the tinkling of coins have since been heard from his bedroom, a small room above the bar.

In 1982 several parapsychologists studied the old inn. One researcher, a lady, was in the bar with two locals when she heard footsteps overhead. On inspection they found nobody there. Her colleague however slept in the haunted bedroom without disturbance.

Incidentally at least two other residents have met violent deaths over the years. There is definitely a feeling, albeit indescribable, about this house.

THE WAGON AND HORSES
WALHAMPTON, Nr LYMINGTON

Walhampton is virtually a suburb of Lymington. It is true that it is divided from the town by a river but to all intents and purposes it is part of Lymington. Walhampton is discovered by following the car ferry signs from the town centre. It possesses a school, some fine houses and The Wagon and Horses which is situated some 200 yards from the Isle of Wight ferry terminal.

The Wagon and Horses is a popular sign and is obviously conducive with country living. It is commemorative of the wagon that collected the field workers at the end of the day to drive them home or to the nearest pub, whichever they preferred.

In 1893, a local character, a gamekeeper named Henry Card, shot himself on the premises. It was a pure accident. Another gamekeeper had been found slain in a nearby woods. The unfortunate man had been shot in the back of the head with his own gun. Foul play was suspected but Henry was demonstrating how it could have happened accidentally. Before an attentive crowd, Henry showed how a man could involuntarily shoot himself from behind. The demonstration was a great success, but, unfortunately for the gamekeeper the gun that he perceived to be unloaded was, in fact, not. Henry Card slumped lifelessly to the floor.

Since that ill-fated night, over one hundred years ago, any inexplicable noise or any vaguely suspect sight has been subscribed to the hapless gamekeeper.

Little or nothing has been witnessed of late but I am told several locals expected to see something on the anniversary in 1993. Whatever they expected to witness, I am assured they did not

THE ROUNDABOUTS
WALLINGTON

Situated on a massive and extremely busy roundabout, with views of a vast viaduct and the sea, this attractive pub has a mischievous ghost.

The spirit is that of a young boy of about twelve or thirteen years of age. His clothes are old fashioned, a black jacket with white trousers and black shoes with gold buckles. He is described as having blond hair and an impish grin.

He sounds to me like a naval cadet or midshipman of the Dana and Marryat era. Probably proudly showing off his uniform. Nearby Fareham was once the most fashionable residence of naval officers.

This spirited young man had quite a prolific number of appearances in the late 1970's but since then he has become a little shy and appears only on rare occasions.

THE CHEQUERS
WELL

For an explanation of 'The Chequers' signboard please refer to the Crookham entry.

The Hamlet of Well has been bypassed by most of the Hampshire guide books. I can only surmise that there was or is a spring or well in the vicinity.

I thought it was time to visit The Chequers. The last time that I was there was in 1960. I was 16 and had cycled the 20 miles from my home. Much that I remembered has changed. The side road that one takes from the Alton – Odiham road has been much widened. The pub itself has been much extended.

On entering, one can still absorb the atmosphere, but as in the vogue, the majority of the establishment has been given over to a dining area.

I had no idea The Chequers was haunted until I chanced to see an episode of 'The Village' on television. The programme actually deals with the village of Bentley, several miles from Well. The Chequers was mentioned because a couple of live-in barmaids had had several disquieting experiences here.

The following episode, which I admit I did not see, featured the appearance of a medium. I am led to believe that the good ladies' examination proved to be inconclusive.

THE ECLIPSE INN
WINCHESTER

f it would have been futile for me to do a brief pen portrait on the town of Southampton, it would be totally banal of me to undertake such a venture in Winchester. This ancient town, steeped in history, has been the subject of many volumes. I shall therefore restrict myself to a spiritual pub crawl around the town.

The sign of The Eclipse is not easily explained. It is unlikely that it has anything to do with an historical eclipse of the sun. It might however be suggestive of one king or dynasty being overtaken or eclipsed by another. As this happened a great many times in the history of England, it would be extremely difficult to pinpoint which particular incident The Eclipse of Winchester commemorates. There was also a famous racehorse named Eclipse that was bred by the Duke of Cumberland. It is no doubt responsible for several Eclipse's in the country but I very much doubt it has any bearing on the Winchester inn.

The Eclipse at Winchester was once the rectory of the Church of St Lawrence but, as my religious knowledge is extremely limited, I have no idea if the sign has any ecclesiastical signification.

Dame Alice Lisle lived in the beautiful New Forest hamlet of Ellingham. She shared the stately Elizabethan mansion Moyles Court with her husband John and two daughters. John Lisle was one of the judges that sentenced Charles Stuart to death. Many years before he had also sentenced a rebel John Penruddock to a similar fate. It was later to be the rebel's son Colonel Penruddock who was to prove instrumental in the terrible demise of Dame Alice in 1685.

Judge Lisle was himself murdered in 1676. His widow Alice was charged at Winchester some 9 years later. The charge being that after the battle of Sedgemoor she had harboured two dissenting ministers named Hickes and Nelthorp. These gentlemen had been unwise enough to throw in their lot with Monmouth in his unsuccessful attempt at seizing the Crown.

Enter the vengeful Colonel Penruddock. He had long suspected Dame Lisle of being a rebel sympathiser and had her house watched by a villager. As soon as he had sufficient evidence he had her arrested.

Whether Alice knew that Hickes and Nelthorp were rebels will never be known. She claimed that she didn't but she was unfortunate enough to appear before the infamous Judge Jeffries who bullied the jury into a conviction. He then sentenced Alice to be dragged on a hurdle to Winchester, there to be burned alive. The horrified clergy of the cathedral begged Judge Jeffries to postpone the execution for five days. By that time they had persuaded James II to change the penalty to death by decapitation.

On September 4th 1685, 71 year old Dame Alice Lisle was taken from prison and lodged at The Eclipse in readiness for her execution the following day. It is said that she was made to leave the inn by an upstairs bedroom window onto a scaffold where the axeman waited. There is a plaque in the square marking the site of her execution.

One would have thought that if ever there were an opportunity for a 'head under the arm, Anne Boleyn archetypical ghost' then this was it, but no, the spiritual grey lady (reputedly Alice Lisle) who inhabits the top bedroom of The Eclipse has her head firmly attached to her body.

Grey ladies are the most prolific inhabitants of the spiritual world, even surpassing monks and highwaymen. Whether The Eclipse's unrested spirit is that of Dame Alice Lisle we will never know. She may have been some poor, equally abused, but less famous lady. There must have been many in this ancient inn's history.

HYDE TAVERN
WINCHESTER

The Hyde Tavern is named after Hyde Abbey that once stood by Winchester's North Gate. The abbey proudly boasted the interned bones of Alfred the Great. Unfortunately, Hyde Abbey was pulled down in the 18th century to make room for a new Bridewell. The remains of England's greatest King were lost forever.

The Hyde Tavern, arguably the oldest inn in Winchester, has a ghost that disturbs sleepers by pulling the blankets off the beds. Sometimes the sleeper is undisturbed but on awakening sees his bed linen in the middle of the floor.

The Hyde Tavern also has a phantom nudger that has a habit of placing a cold hand on some unfortunate's shoulder. The phantom (usually unseen) is thought to be that of an old lady who was denied sustenance one winter and then crept away to perish from cold and hunger.

THE ROYAL HOTEL
WINCHESTER

*W*inchester's *attractive Royal Hotel occupies the site of an ancient convent. Once again we are inflicted by the inevitable spiritual monks and nuns. The hotel definitely has an atmosphere, mysterious but not unpleasant.*

The haunting, tolerably well authenticated over the years, takes place outside the hotel. It is a procession of mumbling (possibly praying) monks and nuns.

Fellow authors, probably more knowledgeable than yours truly, cast doubt on this apparition for the supposedly logical reason that the monastic sexes never mixed. I took it upon myself, out of pure cussedness to research this point. In fact the sexes did mix, seldom I will admit, but possibly this is one of these rare occasions. Possibly an important death, a penance or a protest. All very long ago

ROYAL OAK
WINCHESTER

For an explanation of the 'Royal Oak' sign board please refer to the Langstone entry.

Unfortunately, this magnificent old pub has recently become yet another victim of the chain gangs. The groups that buy up the oldest and most attractive of our pubs and then filter off every last piece of originality and atmosphere.

Thankfully, the outside of the Royal Oak has been little altered over the years. It holds ancient majesty, and ancient the Royal Oak is indeed. It is arguably the oldest licensed premises in the county. The cellar possesses a Saxon wall and 12th century beams.

The haunting, if haunting there be, comes from just outside the pub in Royal Oak Passage. It is an infrequently witnessed group of chanting monks. Hampshire seems to have nearly as many chanting monks as it has phantom Cavaliers. I often wonder if they do the rounds as a tourist attraction, much as morris dancers do in the summer.

I have found nobody in Winchester who has witnessed this particular phenomenon, but, as is often the case sever-

al people that knew people, that knew people who had.

I believe that this is a deeply atmospheric and thought provoking site, especially in the evening when it is a less busy pedestrian thoroughfare. Could it be, I wonder, that if phantoms do not exist here, it would be a necessity to invent them.

THE BEAUCLERK ARMS
(Now Regrettably Woody's)
WINCHFIELD

For many years this establishment, opposite Winchfield Station, rejoiced in the name of the Beauclerk Arms. It was named after a well respected local family. Recently it has suffered from the blasé vogue of the breweries to adopt new trendy names. This practice once more proves that all change is not progress.

Having written columns in many national and local publications on the supernatural it has been my encumbrance to receive many phone calls from people who have experienced inexplicable incidents. The purporters of these experiences range from extremely level headed and serious to the ever present lunatic fringe.

Some years ago a gentleman phoned me who seemed very sincere indeed. He seemed a little self conscience, possibly afraid of mockery. He wondered if I could throw any light on a spectral appearance he and a friend had witnessed as they were leaving the Beauclerk Arms. The gist of the gentleman's story was as follows;

He and a friend were leaving the Beauclerk Arms one evening when they noticed across the road an old Ford Popular saloon. This being the mid 1980's

1ST MAN. "DON'T SEE MANY OLD POPULAR CARS THESE DAYS"

2ND MAN "No!, THEY ARE DISAPPEARING FAST"

the gentlemen were a little surprised to see a vehicle, very popular in the '30's, '40's and '50's but virtually unknown at that time. In the 1980's the sight of such a vehicle was unusual but hardly unique. They were still a favourite with collectors.

As the gentlemen went over to admire the perfectly maintained vehicle it started moving silently away. The Popular travelled some 30 yards down the road, then did a U-turn. It travelled back towards the two witnesses but on it's way it completely disappeared, leaving two very astonished spectators. I listened to this gentleman's story with interest. I had no doubt that he had been sober during the experience and was sincere when relating it to me. I was sorry

that at the time I could not enlighten the gentleman with any explanation whatsoever. Over the years I have heard this story on several other occasions. However, it was always second or third hand and whether they were reports on the tale of the original gentleman or other sightings it was impossible to distinguish.

In the early 1990's I was researching a book on local murders. On August 7th 1935, Arthur Mortimer, a 27 year-old lance-corporal from Aldershot, deliberately knocked a lady off her bike at Stratfield Saye. Not content with this he reversed back, apologised and then blatantly struck the lady, loosening her front teeth. He then calmly drove away.

Before abandoning the stolen car Arthur repeated the practice at Hartley Wintney. Using the same modus operandi he knocked a second young lady from her bicycle. However, before striking her he received such a lashing from her tongue that he retreated forthwith.

The following morning Mortimer was bright and early stealing a vehicle from Farnborough. The car, a rather smart Ford Popular, was Mortimer's choice as he drove the Hants and Surrey lanes looking for potential victims. It was not long before Mortimer passed a couple of young ladies riding their bicycles at Winchfield. Full of cold calculation and yet fired with the prospect of a new prize the young corporal passed the two young ladies and turned off towards Winchfield Station. Near the Beauclerk Arms, Arthur watched the ladies in his rear-view mirror. As they passed the top of the road,

just where it is at it's most narrow at the bridge crossing the railway line, he did a U-turn and followed them.

Twenty year-old Phylis Oakes was riding behind her sister, Betty, when she was struck from behind by a Ford Popular. She bounced off the bonnet and cracked her skull. Despite the screamings and beseeching of her sister, the driver calmly drove away. Shortly after Phylis Oakes died of her injuries.

By this time a pattern was emerging and the police were keen to interview Mortimer. Later on the day when poor Phylis became a victim Mortimer was once again indulging in his pastime, this time over the Surrey boarder at Knaphill. He had knocked a lady from her bicycle, left her unconscious and stolen her money from her handbag. A police chase followed this incident and Mortimer was arrested after crashing into a road block at Guildford.

Arthur Mortimer was tried and convicted at Winchester. He was sentenced to hang for the murder of Phylis Oakes. A sentence that was later changed to a life sentence in a criminal lunatic asylum.

Was there any connection between Mortimer and the phantom Popular. It is a tenuous and somewhat unlikely connection to say the least. Once again, I shall leave it to the readers' discretion.

PS. I have a friend who is a trucker. The most down to earth and unimaginative of men one would have thought. As we were driving over Winchford railway bridge one day he turned to me and stated 'I always get the most inexplicable feeling of deep depression as I pass over this bridge but it's gone a few yards down the road'.

I haven't enlightened him. Not as yet anyway.

JOLLY FARMER
WINCHESTER

The Jolly Farmer is obviously a popular sign relating to agriculture. The farmer's jovial countenance suggesting that the soil was rich and fertile in the area.

However, at the Jolly Farmer near Winchester, this whole area has a slightly oppressive, vaguely mysterious atmosphere about it. Possibly its geographical position accounts for this as it was once Gallows Hill, sight of one of Winchester's four places of execution.

The spirit at the Jolly Farmer is said to be that of Henry Whitley who was charged in 1637 with the theft of four capons and three hens. The authorities had but one sentence for such a heinous crime. So poor convicted Henry was doomed to die on the nearby gallows.

Over the years the spirit of the unfortunate miscreant has been blamed for a certain amount of poltergeist activity at the inn. Quite heavy objects have been moved including a weighty washing machine. Henry has also been blamed for a spate of water taps being turned on. This would seem to have happened on many occasions spanning decades of time.

There is a story, albeit far fetched, that the phantom tap turner is in fact the original landlord. It was he who actually stole the above mentioned birds that poor Henry paid the ultimate price for. The mysterious tap turning being a symbolic action, the washing of an innocent mans blood from a guilty man's hands. Unlikely I admit, but it adds another dimension to the story.

CRICKETERS
YATELEY

I am afraid that any supernatural experiences at this rather pleasant hostelry are very tenuous and poorly corroborated.

Recently certain mechanical appliances have been reported as having a will of their own. I believe the glass washer is a participating culprit. Knowing as little about electrics as I do the internal combustion engine, I verge on the side of the sceptics. I personally possess several electrical gadgets that seem to have a will of their own.

Spasmodically I have used The Cricketers for years. It is the home of local jazz players. The sort of dedicated patriot that is born at the age of forty and remains in suspended animation until the age of seventy.

The Cricketers is old but not that old, and much of the premises were once an adjacent cottage. It is a stone's throw from Blackbushe, once London's second airport, but in later years renowned for its Sunday Market. There were in the 1950's, several horrific crashes at the airport, sustaining considerable loss of life, but I don't believe there is even the remotest connection between these events and any supernatural occurrences at The Cricketers. In the early 1960's the then tiny saloon bar adorned by ex-aircraft seats was also the watering hole of many pilots. This however, would seem to be the full extent of any connection between pub and airfield.

There is little more to say except to mention that a German spy was arrested on or near the premises during the war, but then that's another story.